After the Fall: The Future of Global Cooperation

Geneva Reports on the World Economy 14

International Center for Monetary and Banking Studies (ICMB)

International Center for Monetary and Banking Studies
11A Avenue de la Paix
1202 Geneva
Switzerland

Tel: (41 22) 734 9548
Fax: (41 22) 733 3853
Web: www.icmb.ch

Centre for Economic Policy Research

Centre for Economic Policy Research
3rd Floor
77 Bastwick Street
London EC1V 3PZ
UK

Tel: +44 (20) 7183 8801
Fax: +44 (20) 7183 8820
Email: cepr@cepr.org
Web: www.cepr.org

ISBN: 978-1-907142-55-0

After the Fall: The Future of Global Cooperation

Geneva Reports on the World Economy 14

Jeffry Frieden
Harvard University

Michael Pettis
Peking University

Dani Rodrik
Harvard University

Ernesto Zedillo
Yale University

ICMB INTERNATIONAL CENTER
FOR MONETARY
AND BANKING STUDIES
CIMB CENTRE INTERNATIONAL
D'ETUDES MONETAIRES
ET BANCAIRES

About the Authors

Jeffry Frieden is Stanfield Professor of International Peace in Harvard University's Department of Government. He specialises in the politics of international monetary and financial relations. Frieden is the author (with Menzie Chinn) of *Lost Decades: The Making of America's Debt Crisis and the Long Recovery* (2011). Frieden is also the author of *Global Capitalism: Its Fall and Rise in the Twentieth Century* (2006), of *Banking on the World: The Politics of American International Finance* (1987), of *Debt, Development, and Democracy: Modern Political Economy and Latin America, 1965-1985* (1991), and is the editor or co-editor of over a dozen other books on related topics. His articles on the politics of international economic issues have appeared in a wide variety of scholarly and general-interest publications.

Michael Pettis is a professor at Peking University's Guanghua School of Management, where he specializes in Chinese financial markets. He has also taught, from 2002 to 2004, at Tsinghua University's School of Economics and Management and, from 1992 to 2001, at Columbia University's Graduate School of Business.

Pettis has worked on Wall Street in trading, capital markets, and corporate finance since 1987, when he joined the Sovereign Debt trading team at Manufacturers Hanover (now JP Morgan). Most recently, from 1996 to 2001, Pettis worked at Bear Stearns, where he was Managing Director-Principal heading the Latin American Capital Markets and the Liability Management groups.

Dani Rodrik is Rafiq Hariri Professor of International Political Economy at Harvard's John F. Kennedy School of Government. He has published widely in the areas of economic development, international economics, and political economy. His most recent book is *The Globalization Paradox: Democracy and the Future of the World Economy* (2011).

His current research focuses on designing growth strategies for developing economies. In 2007 he was awarded the inaugural Albert O. Hirschman Prize of the Social Sciences Research Council. He is also the recipient of the Leontief Award for Advancing the Frontiers of Economic Thought. His work has been supported by research grants from the Carnegie Corporation, Ford Foundation, and Rockefeller Foundation. He teaches courses on economic development and globalization.

Ernesto Zedillo is the Frederick Iseman '74 Director of the Yale Center for the Study of Globalization; Professor in the Field of International Economics and Politics; Professor of International and Area Studies; and Professor Adjunct of Forestry and Environmental Studies at Yale University. He teaches undergraduate courses at Yale on debating globalisation, trade, and the economic evolution and challenges of the Latin American and Caribbean countries. In Mexico, he was with the Central Bank of Mexico from 1978-1987 then served the National Government as Undersecretary of the Budget, Secretary of the Budget and Economic Planning, Secretary of Education, and President (1994-2000). He holds a PhD in Economics from Yale University. In 2011 he was elected as an international member of the American Philosophical Society. Among his edited books are included *The Future of Globalization: Explorations in Light of Recent Turbulence, Global Warming: Looking Beyond Kyoto* and *Rethinking the "War on Drugs" through the US-Mexico Prism.*

Contents

List of Figures

List of Tables

List of Conference Participants

Edmond Alphandéry   Chairman
CNP Assurances
Paris

Liliana Andonova   Professor of Political Science
The Graduate Institute of International and
Development Studies
Geneva

Richard Apostolik   President
Global Association of Risk Professionals, Inc
USA

Vit Bárta   Advisor to Governor
Czech National Bank
Prague

Rémy Bersier   Member of the Executive Board
Banque Julius Baer & Cie SA
Geneva

Andrea Bianchi   Professor of International Law
The Graduate Institute of International and
Development Studies
Geneva

Thomas Biersteker   Gasteyger Professor of International Security
The Graduate Institute of International and
Development Studies
Geneva

Laurence Boone   Chief Economist
Bank of America Merrill Lynch
Paris

Claudio Borio   Deputy Head Monetary and Economic Department
Director of Research and Statistics
Bank for International Settlements
Basel

Pascal Boris

Head of Territory Switzerland
BNP Paribas (Suisse) SA
Geneva

Luigi Buttiglione

Head of Global Strategy
Brevan Howard Investment Products
Geneva

Vincent Chetail

Associate Professor
The Graduate Institute of International and
Development Studies
Geneva

Andrew Clapham

Professor of International Law
The Graduate Institute of International and
Development Studies
Geneva

Benoît Coeuré

Member of the Executive Board
European Central Bank
Frankfurt am Main

Jean-Pierre Danthine

Vice-chairman of the Governing Board
Swiss National Bank
Zurich

Pierre Darier

Partner
Lombard Odier
Geneva

Alain de Crombrugghe

Visiting Fellow
The Graduate Institute of International and
Development Studies
Geneva

Jacques Delpla

Conseil d'Analyse Economique
Paris

Paul Dembinski

Director
Observatoire de la Finance
Geneva

Andreas Dombret

Member of the Executive Board
Deutsche Bundesbank
Frankfurt am Main

Cédric Dupont

Professor of Political Science
Director, International programmes and Executive
Education
The Graduate Institute of International and
Development Studies
Geneva

Jeffry Frieden

Professor of Government
Harvard University
        Cambridge

Hans Genberg

Assistant Director
Independent Evaluation Office of the IMF
Washington D.C

Stefan Gerlach

Deputy Governor
Central Bank of Ireland
Dublin

Michel Girardin

Member of Senior Management
Union Bancaire Privée

Christos Gortsos

Professor of International Economic Law
Panteion University of Athens
Athens

Takatoshi Ito

Professor
Graduate School of Economics
University of Tokyo

Thomas Jordan

Chairman of the Governing Board
Swiss National Bank
Zürich

Christian Kastrop

Deputy Director General
Bundesministerium der Finanzen
Berlin

Pierre Keller

Former Senior Partner
Lombard Odier
Geneva

Ulrich Kohli

Professorof Economics
University of Geneva

Dino Kos

Managing Director
Hamiltonian Associates, LTD
New York

Signe Krogstrup	Deputy Head of Monetary Analysis Swiss National Bank Zürich
Rajiv Kumar	Director and Chief Executive Indian Council for Research on International Economic Relations (ICRIER)
Anne Le Lorier	Deputy Governor Banque de France Paris
Emmanuelle Merle	Assistant Vice-president Banque Cantonale de Genève Geneva
Maurice Monbaron	Member of the Board Crédit Agricole (Suisse) SA Geneva
John Murray	Deputy Governor Bank of Canada Ottawa
José Ocampo	Professor School of International and Public Affairs Columbia University New York
Katrin Ochsenbein	Economist Macroeconomic Support Division Swiss State Secretariat of Economic Affairs (SECO) Bern
Ugo Panizza	Chief Debt and Finance Analysis Unit UNCTAD Geneva
Yung Chul Park	Professor Division of International Studies Korea University Seoul
Joost Pauwelyn	Professor of International Law The Graduate Institute of International and Development Studies Geneva

Michael Pettis   Senior Associate
                               Carnegie Endowment
                               Beijing

Ivan Pictet   Former Senior Managing Partner
                               Pictet & Cie
                               Geneva

Friederike Pohlenz   Deputy Head Section
                               Multilateral Affairs
                               Swiss Federal Department of Finance
                               Bern

Jonas Pontusson   Professor of Political Science
                               University of Geneva

Richard Portes   Professor of Economics
                               London Business School and CEPR

Davide Rodogno   Professor of International History
                               The Graduate Institute of International and
                               Development Studies
                               Geneva

Dani Rodrik   Rafiq Hariri Professor of International Political
                               Economy
                               Harvard University
                               Cambridge

Barbara Roos   Member of Senior Management
                               Notenstein Private Bank Ltd
                               Geneva

Salvatore Rossi   Member of the Governing Board
                               Bank of Italy
                               Rome

Jean-Pierre Roth   Chairman
                               Banque Cantonale de Genève
                               Geneva

Amlan Roy   Managing Director, Head of Global Demographic and
                               Pensions
                               Fixed Income Research Department
                               Crédit Suisse
                               London

Hans-Joerg Rudloff   Chairman
                               Barclays Capital
                               London

Neal Soss

Chief Economist
Crédit Suisse
New-York

Claudia Stirboeck

Head of Office of Board Member
Deutsch Bundesbank
Frankfurt am Main

Alexander Swoboda

Professor of Economics Emeritus
The Graduate Institute of International and
Development Studies
Geneva

Cédric Tille

Professor of International Economics
The Graduate Institute of International and
Development Studies
Geneva

Marc Uzan

Executive Director
Reinventing Bretton Woods Committee
Paris

Xin Wang

Chief Representative
People's Bank of China
Frankfurt Office

Pawel Wyczanski

Advisor
Financial System
National Bank of Poland
Warsaw

Charles Wyplosz

Professor of International Economics
The Graduate Institute of International and
Development Studies, Geneva
Director ICMB, Geneva
CEPR, London

Jean Zwahlen

Senior Adviser for Asia
Union Bancaire Privée
Geneva

Acknowledgements

The authors are grateful to the discussants and to the participants at the Geneva Conference of May 2012, where a preliminary version of the present report was presented and carefully discussed. Particular thanks go to Menzie Chinn, Barry Eichengreen, Marina Ivanova and Haynie Wheeler. The discussion section has been prepared by Salvatore Dell'Erba and Katja Mann. Many thanks as well to Laurence Procter who singlehandedly organised the conference and performed all of the background work behind this report.

Foreword

International cooperation has been a recurrent theme in each of the thirteen Geneva Reports on the World Economy published by CEPR and ICMB since 1999. The 2004 report, *International Economic and Financial Cooperation: New Issues, New Actors, New Responses*, analysed this issue in some depth. This report, the fourteenth in the series, picks up this issue once again, but this time the approach is different, the recommendations more cautious and incremental, and the prognosis bleaker. This is not surprising: the authors demonstrate very clearly why international cooperation is difficult at the best of times, and very difficult indeed in the midst of a severe financial crisis.

A comparison of the 2012 and the 2004 reports shows clearly what has and has not changed as a result of the crisis. The 2004 report was very much concerned with the machinery of international cooperation, and it argued, very persuasively, for a new set of institutions, including a G4, comprising the US, the Eurozone, Japan and China; and a larger Council for International Financial and Economic Cooperation, comprising no more than 15 members. A G4 has not emerged, although the coordinated crisis management by the Fed, the ECB, the Bank of Japan and the Bank of England resembled a central bankers' G4. The G20 which emerged from the burst of cooperation at the beginning of the crisis is in many ways a somewhat larger version of the Council proposed in the 2004 report. Whether the G20 can sustain its early momentum is less clear, however. Chapter 4 of this report, which analyses the experiences of cooperation in recent years, offers a number of reasons to be pessimistic.

The latest report looks at international cooperation from a different perspective; it devotes less attention to the question of institutional machinery, focusing instead on identifying the issues that are most likely to benefit from cooperation, and on which the international community should focus its efforts. The authors' argument is very clear: international cooperation is difficult at the best of times, and these are not the best of times. Governments in the developed countries, beset by all manner of economic and financial difficulties, lack the political capital to spend on international cooperation; the demands of their domestic constituencies are too pressing. Governments in the large emerging economies may be under less domestic political pressure and so more inclined to cooperate, but they have very different incentives from their developed country counterparts. Cooperative agreements may therefore be difficult in general, and impossible in some areas. Given this analysis, the authors' recommendation is logical and compelling. Since improving international cooperation will be very difficult for the foreseeable future, governments should concentrate their efforts on that issues where the gains are likely to be larger and the difficulties smaller. More precisely, progress is likely to be more difficult in trade policy and financial regulation, and the gains are likely to be smaller; governments should spend their political capital on other issues instead. They should focus on improving macroeconomic policy coordination as a means of preventing a resurgence of the global imbalances that helped trigger the crisis. The only way progress can be achieved is by focusing on a one key issue.

Not every reader will agree, but that is not the point. The aim of the Geneva Reports is to stimulate informed discussion and debate on issues that matter. This the authors have achieved, and we are grateful to them for their diligence and dedication. We are also grateful to the CEPR Publications team – Anil Shamdasani and Charlie Anderson – for the smooth and professional way in which they have prepared the report for publication.

Charles Wyplosz   Stephen Yeo
Director, ICMB   Chief Executive Officer, CEPR

18 July 2012

1 Introduction: Past Imperfect, Present Tense, Future Conditional

The world economy faces its most serious test since the 1930s. The financial crisis that began in 2007 has yet to run its course: in most of the OECD, the recovery is at best halting, while much of the European Union has collapsed into a second recession and faces a daunting sovereign debt burden, the threat of severe banking crises and the possibility of a break-up of the monetary union. Emerging markets have done better, but their fortunes remain closely connected to trends in the developed world. The immediate future of global economic activity is not promising.

The longer-term future of the international economic order is also in doubt. Even if the principal economies were to resolve their current financial problems without another major disaster, the world economy confronts substantial challenges. The lack of policy coordination that facilitated the macroeconomic imbalances that led to the crisis still prevails, raising the possibility of a new round of debt accumulation and debt crises. The international financial system has demonstrated a fragility that threatens the global economy more generally. Even as more and more developing countries turn to exports to drive their economic growth, the appetite of the developed world for these imports seems to be waning. International financial flows remain at an extraordinarily high level, but there are enduring questions both about whether they contribute as hoped to a more efficient allocation of resources, and about whether they can be sustained without creating another round of bubbles and crashes.

Many of these problems require concerted international efforts to address them. Calls for better 'global governance' reflect the accurate perception that global markets seem to have exceeded the ability of national governments, or ad hoc international cooperation, to address the problems to which they may give rise.

And yet the structure of international cooperation on economic issues seems seriously deficient. On some dimensions, such as central bank cooperation, it appears to have worked reasonably well in difficult times.[1] But this relative success is almost entirely limited to monetary policy, including specific interventions of

---

1   Although some emerging-market governments, such as those of Brazil and China, have complained that excessively loose monetary policy in the OECD was 'exporting inflation' to the rest of the world.

lending of last resort. On virtually every other important global economic issue, international cooperation is stalled, flawed or non-existent.

We do not think the very limited successes of attempts at greater global economic governance, although regrettable, are surprising. There are major barriers to expanding the realm of international cooperation. This is especially true in the very difficult circumstances of the aftermath of the greatest economic crisis in several generations.

Four interrelated factors make international economic cooperation difficult. First, normative theory is only favourable to global governance in a qualified way, depending upon whether or not international collective action is truly essential to provide the desired public good. Second, even where the case for collective action is strong, governments face substantial domestic political obstacles to participation in global cooperative enterprises. Third, there are substantial divergences among the goals and attitudes of the major international economic players. And, finally, the recent history of cooperative efforts is not particularly encouraging.

The immediate future path of international economic affairs will indeed be complicated by the fact that the major centres of economic activity are likely to spend much of the coming decade absorbed in difficult attempts to clean up the refuse of the financial crisis, and to find new patterns of economic growth. As North America, Europe and Japan struggle with their own domestic economic and political problems, they are unlikely to be willing or able to expend much effort to deal with matters outside their borders even if, for the medium and long term, it is in their own national interest to do so. Past experience and common sense show that domestic political support is a prerequisite of meaningful international engagement. A government that cannot count on its constituents to support its foreign policies will soon either change its policies, or cease to be in government. Partly as a consequence of politicians' failure to communicate to their constituencies the benefits of international cooperation, there appears to be limited public support for the measures necessary to expand it.

At the same time, the number and character of the relevant international economic actors is changing. It is hard to imagine serious discussions about trade, finance or exchange rates without including China, Brazil and other emerging economies. However, the major emerging economies are at very different places on the path to global economic and political engagement. Generally, it is not clear that such countries as China, India and Brazil will be willing, able or allowed anytime soon to take a leading role in the management of international economic problems – for one thing, their interests and perspectives are likely to be very different from those of the incumbents. Even among the emerging economies themselves, there are important differences in interests and perspectives that reflect divergent economic and political structures, conflicting positions in the global economy and even, in some cases, a history of mutual suspicion. The expanding number of systemically important nations increases both the need for substantive cooperation to include those nations, and the difficulty of achieving consensus among ever more disparate international actors.

As the world struggles to emerge from the most serious crisis since the Great Depression of the 1930s, then, we must also think about the more distant future. What are likely to be the principal issues facing the international economy over the next decade? What could a realistic analysis hope for in the way of progress in confronting the problems of the future? What are the constraints imposed by the realities of international and domestic politics? And, most directly for our purposes, what forms of international economic cooperation are the most important to pursue, and most likely to be achieved?[2]

In what follows, we speculate on these matters. We start, in Chapter 2, with a quick summary of some of the lessons of previous experiences with an integrated international economy. In Chapter 3, we move to an overview of the current situation. We outline the major dangers facing the world economy in the near term, and the political and economic stumbling blocks to their resolution. Chapter 4 summarises the recent experience of cooperative ventures in a world made more complicated by the entry of new major players, and the persistence of conflicts of interest and perspectives among the principal powers. Despite continued rhetorical commitments to economic cooperation – many falling far short of any meaningful global governance – the recent history of actual attempts to implement such cooperation is very chequered, and largely disappointing. Chapter 5 analyses some of the domestic economic and political obstacles that explain the limited scope of cooperative ventures. It also argues that the major players are likely to face continuing domestic political constraints over the coming decade. All governments require support from their constituents to undertake potentially costly international initiatives; without this support, such international initiatives will face grave difficulties. In Chapter 6, we discuss what normative theory would suggest might be desirable in the way of governance structures to address the global problems outlined in the previous chapters. We ask what sorts of international cooperative measures, institutionalised or otherwise, might be advantageous, assuming they are attainable. We argue that the great efforts required to achieve forward movement warrant that the international community concentrate on limited but very important issues, topics in which the normative case for global governance is particularly strong. Chapter 7 assumes that the worst-case scenarios are avoided and attempts to sketch the general state of international economic affairs five to seven years from now. We attempt to identify the issues that we think will be central to this new phase in the international economic order. Chapter 8 summarises and concludes.

We emphasise that cooperation among national governments over global economic problems is more important in certain areas than in others.[3] But

---

2   Two previous Geneva Reports have focused closely on related issues in international cooperation: De Gregorio *et al* (1999) and Kenen *et al* (2004).

3   The scholarly literature in International Relations typically distinguishes between cooperation and coordination. The former implies a Prisoner's Dilemma or similar game, with a Nash equilibrium that allows for a Pareto superior Nash bargaining solution, towards which governments can work. The latter implies something like an Assurance game, in which governments agree on converging on a focal point, although different focal points may have different welfare and distributional effects. For our purposes, we elide the two definitions; different issue areas may fall into one or the other category, and in any case the classification is sometimes controversial. Indeed, many scholars believe that interstate bargaining *always* involves both cooperation and coordination. An influential statement is Fearon (1998).

where macroeconomic spillovers are concerned, it is both vital, and difficult to achieve. National political systems do not easily set aside important domestic problems to focus on more remote international ones; and the preferences of both broad publics and powerful special interests in different nations are often at odds. This is especially the case in the context of a difficult recovery from a wrenching crisis. It is also especially the case when there are actors on the international economic scene who have gradually moved from the periphery of global economic developments towards the centre, and whose concerns are often radically different both from each other's, and from those of the traditional economic powers.

Given the undoubted difficulty of achieving substantial international cooperation, we emphasise the need to focus efforts on where they are most required, and most likely to succeed. This leads us to undertake a normative analysis of the argument for greater global governance, and to argue for incremental rather than radical objectives. We also try to identify the issues of greatest prominence, and on which cooperation is both most important and most feasible; we focus on macroeconomic policy coordination, including attention to global imbalances. We regard these as important to future international economic stability; there are good arguments in favour of international cooperation to deal with them; and there is some political support for movement in this direction.

Our conclusions are rarely rosy, and may appear pessimistic. We prefer to think that we are realistic, and guardedly optimistic. It is, after all, better to confront the obstacles we face than to ignore them.

2 The Ghost of Globalisation Past: Lessons for Globalisation Present

2.1 Globalisation past

We can look to history for some guidance as to the problems the world economy is likely to face.[4] Indeed, the world has been here before. For decades before 1914, the international economy was roughly as integrated as it is today. Scholars disagree about just how integrated it was, and is, but all indications are that goods and capital moved around the world very easily between 1870 and 1914 – not as quickly or cheaply as they do today, but with as few explicit government controls. In fact, on a couple of dimensions the world economy was more 'globalised' then than now. There was an international monetary order that tied almost all major countries together in something approaching a monetary union. By the early 20th century every economy of any significance, except China and Persia, was on the gold standard, which facilitated trade, investment and travel in important ways. By the same token, international migration was much freer then than it is today: Europeans, at least, could migrate to much of the New World with no documents at all.

That first era of globalisation, propelled by the industrial revolution and economic liberalism, was remarkably successful by the standards of the economic development achieved at the time. The world economy grew more in the 75 years before 1914 than it had in the previous 750, and there was substantial convergence among countries of the core and lands of recent settlement. Some poor and middle-income countries moved towards the living standards of the early industrialisers, although the world was divided between an industrial core and a resource-exporting periphery. Macroeconomic conditions were relatively stable, despite periodic crises and 'panics', as were prices. None of this is to ignore the uglier sides of the period – colonialism, authoritarian governments, agrarian crises and grinding urban poverty were all parts of the 19th and early 20th century world order. Nonetheless, compared to what had come before – and what came immediately after – this was a flourishing global economy.

---

4   The classic statement, with regard to international monetary relations, is Eichengreen (1996). See also Frieden (2006).

2.2   Globalisation collapsed

And yet that globalised economy came to a grinding halt in 1914. After WWI was over, the world's political and economic leaders attempted to restore the classical order that had prevailed for so long – and they failed. It was not for lack of trying, as conferences, meetings, treaties and international organisations proliferated as never before. But nothing worked; the global economy fragmented and eventually, after the 1929 downturn hit, broke down into trade and currency wars, and eventually shooting wars.

The interwar economy started off on a promising note. After a surprisingly fast few years of reconstruction, by 1922 international trade and finance had resumed at something resembling their prewar pace. The central financial nexus of the era was the flow of capital from the world's leading surplus country, the US, to borrowers in central and eastern Europe, Germany in particular. This particular 'macroeconomic imbalance' helped speed the return to something approaching normalcy on both sides of the Atlantic, as American industry and finance boomed and the German economy recovered rapidly.

The weaknesses of the interwar settlement were revealed after recession began in 1929. Cooperation among the principal economic players broke down quickly. The French and Germans continued to spar over every aspect of their relationship, infusing even purely financial issues with the venom of their diplomatic conflicts. Some hoped that the new economic powerhouse, the US, would contribute to a resolution of the problems, especially since the US had become the world's principal creditor nation. Yet US citizens preferred to stand aside from European affairs, both because they were preoccupied with the country's own problems and because their political system was dominated by economic nationalists and isolationists who objected on principle to subordinating national concerns to global cooperation. One source of US reticence is of contemporary relevance: many Americans felt that existing international organisations did not accurately reflect the role of the US in the world, and were indeed to some extent intended to constrain US influence in favour of the European powers.

As the world economy stagnated and spiralled downwards, domestic affairs loomed ever larger in the concerns of other national governments as well. By 1934 every semblance of international economic cooperation had disappeared. Trade wars, currency wars, and eventually shooting wars ensued.

2.3   Lessons from the past

There are two principal lessons of that previous age of international economic integration and its collapse after 1918. First, an open international economy requires the purposive collaboration of the major economic powers, especially during periods of economic stress. The 19th-century fiction of self-equilibrating international markets may have applied to particular markets; but it did not apply to the world economy as a whole. For a globalised economy to persist, especially in the face of periodic crises, the principal financial centres need to cooperate to stabilise markets and safeguard openness.[5]

The second lesson of the collapse of the classical version of globalisation is that national governments will be unable to undertake the measures needed to sustain an open economy if they do not have the support of their constituents. Policymakers must answer to their constituents – who might be narrow elites or broad masses – and if constituents are hostile to the world economy, policymakers who ignore this hostility will be pushed out of office. Many of the major powers of the 19th century were at least partially undemocratic; they did not need to answer to the demands of the middle and working classes. By the 1920s, this had changed, and almost every industrial country was democratic. A failure to reflect accurately the interests of constituents led, quickly, to a powerful backlash – both against the government, and often against the rest of the world.

Past successes, and failures, of globalisation demonstrate that a functioning, open, international economy requires some degree of cooperation among nations, especially among the major economic centres. They also demonstrate that cooperation in turn requires domestic political support for the measures necessary to help keep the world economy functioning smoothly. How does the current situation look, in the context of these lessons?

---

5   To be sure, the view expressed here – drawn largely from Eichengreen (1996) – has been challenged to some extent. See, for example, Flandreau (1997).

3   The Current Situation

3.1   Introduction

The past 30 years have been an extraordinary period in international economic history. After a very troubled decade in the 1970s, the 1980s saw the developed countries gradually resolve to redouble their engagement with one another, and with the world economy. Over the course of the 1980s, most developing countries followed suit, turning away from semi-autarkic policies of import substitution and pushing their producers into world markets. China and Vietnam also joined the world economy, turning their communist-ruled nations away from central planning and towards a hybrid form of open-economy state capitalism. After 1989, in the most striking shift, the Soviet Union collapsed, and its successor states and former allies also joined the international economic order.

Globalisation in full had arrived anew, the Cold War was over and capitalism had won. Rapid economic growth in China and India raised the possibility of real convergence between poor and rich countries. Macroeconomic conditions stabilised as inflation came down almost everywhere and recessions were infrequent and mild – so much so that there was talk of a 'Great Moderation'.

All this was interrupted by the global crisis that began in 2007. Since then, the world has struggled with a continuing series of related financial and economic emergencies. In their attempts to address the effects of the crisis and its aftermath, every major economy has been, and is likely to continue to be, deeply absorbed in its own domestic (and, in the case of the European Union, regional) difficulties. This in itself poses a problem for attempts at international cooperation, as the resolution of national (or regional) difficulties takes precedence over attempts to deal with more distant global concerns.

3.2   A world out of balance

The various crises that have peppered the ongoing Great Recession – the American financial meltdown, the Eurozone debt disaster, financial stress in other parts of Europe – have many and complex causes. Innovative and risky financial instruments and inadequate financial regulation certainly played a role. For our purposes, what are particularly relevant are the sources of the crisis that involve international interrelationships, and in particular, macroeconomic linkages among countries. One indication of these linkages has been the emergence of 'global imbalances', large-scale surpluses and deficits among countries. For the better part of a decade, trillions of dollars flowed from surplus countries – largely in northern Europe, East Asia and the Middle East – towards deficit countries, especially the US, the UK and peripheral Europe (Ireland as well as southern, central and eastern Europe). In the new post-crisis atmosphere, many of these deficits will be difficult or impossible to sustain. Over the next several years, both deficit and surplus countries alike will be absorbed with the difficult task of 'rebalancing', adjusting to an environment in which deficits in most cases will of necessity have to be smaller – and, as a result, so too will surpluses.

There is nothing inherently wrong with trade and current account deficits and surpluses, and nor do they necessarily lead to crisis. In any well-functioning global economy there will be imbalances in trade and financial flows. In fact, capital should move from places where its marginal productivity is lower to places where its marginal productivity is higher. There have been many instances, such as in the US for much of the 19th century, in which trade imbalances persist for years with few difficulties.

Trade deficits, and their counterpart, capital inflows, are desirable to the extent that the process is associated with productive investment in the deficit (borrowing) country. Rapidly growing nations – such as the US and the other Areas of Recent Settlement in the 19th century – typically run trade deficits and import capital as they grow. The deficits can be reversed, and the loans repaid, to the extent that the borrowed funds (and imported equipment) go directly or indirectly to investments that increase the productive capacity of the country, and its ability to export to earn the resources necessary to service the debts.

Problems arise when foreign borrowing goes to current consumption, or to other purposes that do not increase productivity. In some instances, national policies encourage capital flows that are hard to justify on purely economic grounds. In other instance, the ready availability of foreign funds provides a permissive environment for public or private actions with potentially detrimental effects on the economy as a whole. In the most recent set of capital flow cycles, large-scale borrowing was often associated with risky behaviour on the part of borrowers and lenders, lax regulation, and asset bubbles. Scholars are likely to argue for a long time about the exact causal processes at work, but one thing seems unquestionable: the capital flows of the past decade led to systemic problems at the domestic and international levels.

The most recent boom-and-bust cycle reminds us that financial flows, if poorly managed, can impose very substantial negative externalities. There are externalities at home, as a country's borrowers (or lenders) can end up presenting taxpayers with the bill for a costly bailout. There are externalities abroad, as the loss of confidence that comes with a financial crisis can be transmitted to neighbouring, or similar, nations.

These problems are aggravated by the absence of global institutions that can moderate the effects of capital-flow reversals. This was seen in the case of the 'global imbalances' of the past decade. The US borrowed to finance a Federal budget deficit that was not justified on economic grounds, and to fund a housing boom and bubble. The pattern was similar in the UK. In most of peripheral Europe, deficits were also associated with a surge of spending on consumption; most of the investment financed went to the non-tradables sectors – especially housing. Overall, the vast majority of the borrowing connected to these imbalances went towards government or household consumption.[6] At the same time, in both lending and borrowing nations there appear to have been serious holes in the framework of financial regulation, holes that created excessive moral hazard or otherwise exposed national governments to serious threats. These facts – that so few of the trillions of dollars in foreign investment and lending went to augment national productive investment, and that financial regulation appears to have been so lax – are at the root of the continuing problems. Now both deficit and surplus nations have to adjust to a new reality, in a process of 'deleveraging' that is at the heart of the economic dilemmas raised by the aftermath of the global financial crisis.

3.3   The politics of adjustment

The political problems are perhaps even more daunting than the purely economic ones. Every debt crisis is followed by conflict over the distribution of the adjustment burden.[7] When, as in the current case, cross-border debts are at issue, there are two dimensions of conflict. First, creditor countries and debtor countries square off to see which will undertake the bulk of the costly adjustment: creditors demand debtor austerity to maintain debt service, while debtors demand a debt restructuring to make the debt more manageable. Typically, some compromise is worked out – after all, both sides have an incentive to reach agreement – but the battle over the compromise can be hard-fought and drawn out.

A second dimension of conflict usually erupts *within* countries, over who domestically will be asked to contribute to deal with the debt overhang. In creditor countries, for example, the question might be whether it will be financial institutions or taxpayers. In debtor countries, the issue is the distributional incidence of the austerity measures necessary to maintain debt service: taxpayers or beneficiaries of government services, workers or managers, the private or the public sector. Historical precedent suggests that if the political elite does not address these distributional problems directly and forcefully, the result can be the rise of radical political parties of the left and right that seize the debate (Simmons, 1997). Debt crises are never resolved easily; they always lead to substantial international and domestic political tension. The current crisis and its aftermath have been no exception, and in some instances the tension has only just begun to manifest itself.

The two principal foci of the crisis that began in 2007, and their ongoing effects, are symptomatic of the great economic and political difficulties we face in dealing with their enduring impact. The first is the series of intra-Eurozone debt crises that continue to bedevil the European economy. The second involves

---

6   See Chinn and Frieden (2011) for a survey.
7   Eichengreen (1996) makes this argument convincingly about the analogous problems of the 1920s and 1930s.

the US, although some of its most daunting dilemmas can best be seen from the standpoint of such surplus nations as China and Japan.

3.4   Europe on edge

The crisis affecting Europe has its origins in macroeconomic divergences between northern Europe and countries on the European periphery, and resultant capital flows from the north to the periphery (we speak of peripheral Europe to include Ireland and states in eastern and central Europe, many of which were major borrowers and none of which are southern). The process as it unfolded illustrated some of the well-known weaknesses in the design of the euro: the economic heterogeneity of member states of the Eurozone, the absence of common financial regulation in a common financial market, the lack of serious fiscal coordination, the absence of explicit lender of last resort provisions, and the lack of a credible commitment not to bail out member states in trouble.

The principal macroeconomic heterogeneity can be illustrated with the divergence between slow growth in Germany and rapid growth on the periphery. In the 1990s, in the aftermath of German reunification, the country's labour unions, businesses and government agreed to restrain wage growth in order to help the country absorb low-productivity eastern Germany. Coupled with a rapidly ageing population, German policies to restrain wages and consumption drove the already high German savings rate higher. Soon the deficits that had developed after reunification were trade surpluses, which grew dramatically after the introduction of the euro.[8]

Meanwhile, peripheral Europe was growing more rapidly, and both wages and prices were rising more than in Germany (and the rest of northern Europe). The European Central Bank, of course, could not set a monetary policy appropriate both for the slow-growing North and the fast-growing periphery; the monetary policy that developed was probably too tight for the North and too loose for the periphery. The result was what can be regarded as an increasingly depreciated real exchange rate for Germany relative to the rest of Europe, all of which allowed the country to dramatically increase its exports to the rest of Europe, and to the rest of the world. During the decade following the establishment of the euro, Germany's trade surplus was one of the three largest in the world. Exports in fact were responsible for most of German growth during that period. Germany was to the rest of Europe as China was to the rest of the world.

The counterparts to the large German surpluses were trade deficits in peripheral Europe. Before the creation of the euro, Italy, Spain, France, Greece and Portugal had a mixed record on this account – they occasionally ran fairly large trade deficits, and occasionally substantial trade surpluses. Only after monetary union did their trade deficits explode. Rapid growth and rising wages and prices in the periphery – whether due to national policy or to Balassa-Samuelson effects – meant that within the Eurozone Germany's 'currency' was depreciated in real terms while the peripheral 'currency' was appreciated in real terms.

---

8   For a recent reminder, see Artus (2012).

The Spanish situation is illustrative – both because it is perhaps the most important of the Eurozone deficit countries, and because it did not have the features typically associated with the crisis. In the decade before the crisis, Spain had sound fiscal policies, and a relatively prudent and strictly regulated banking system.

Spain matched the German savings-investment surplus with an opposite deficit. The rise of Spanish prices and wages relative to those in Germany made investment in tradables unattractive, so private investment largely went into the non-tradables sector. This primarily took the form of private investment in real estate, aided by the ability of households to take advantage of low interest rates to finance new mortgages. The result was a massive housing boom. There was also a rise in debt-financed current consumption by households. As a result, Spain experienced both a boom in real estate construction and a consumption boom that drove down the domestic savings rate.

Uncertainty about the sustainability of Spanish debt is now so widespread that the government's credit has been impaired, interest rates on Spanish debt have soared, and a significant number of Spanish banks are in need of exceptional support, while both the real estate market and household consumption are in a state of collapse. Spain has been cutting government spending and raising taxes in an effort to reduce consumption and raise savings further. Unemployment has skyrocketed and the prospects are for unemployment to remain at very high levels unless and until either the German stance changes, or domestic wages have adjusted sufficiently. But neither is particularly attractive to Germany, because they effectively force Germany to run a deficit, a position abhorrent to the country's export-oriented manufacturing sector.

The Eurozone (and broader European) crisis is the result of unsustainable borrowing (and lending) – of unsustainable deficits in the periphery and surpluses in the North. We see no particular ethical imbalance here, even in the financial boom and bubble leading to 2008 – after all, it is hard to argue that irresponsible lending is any better than irresponsible borrowing. It is currently popular to emphasise moralising exhortations that Spaniards and Greeks become as virtuous, thrifty and hardworking as Germans. However, both a lasting resolution of the European debt crises, and some hope of avoiding recurrences, depend on the region agreeing on macroeconomic and financial policies that avoid a repetition of these patterns of unsustainable deficits and surpluses.

Resolving the European crisis in an orderly manner will be politically very demanding. Debtor-country governments face major difficulties in imposing austerity measures sufficient to allow them to service their debts – even if these debts are substantially restructured. Adjustment in the surplus countries will also be difficult, and not only because restructured debts impose some costs on creditors. A more lasting resolution of the crisis requires substantial changes in the positions of both debtor and creditor countries; it requires Germany, for example, to raise domestic consumption significantly. The German government could reduce income and consumption taxes so as to increase real disposable household income, but this, in addition to exciting fears of inflation, would likely reduce the trade surplus that Germany has become accustomed to identify as a measure of economic success.

So far, most of the real adjustment that has taken place in the Eurozone has been on the part of the debtors, and then in some more than others. Figure 3.1 shows that only Spain and Ireland have realised a substantial reduction in unit labour costs since 2007, and unit labour costs have not risen in the major surplus countries – in fact, they have declined slightly in Germany. While it may seem unwarranted to fault Germany and other surplus countries for wage restraint, an increase in wages and consumption is the necessary counterpart of a reduction in their surpluses. Figure 3.2 is particularly striking. It shows the massive adjustment undertaken in such non-Eurozone deficit countries as Bulgaria, Lithuania and Latvia, which have effectively eliminated current account deficits that a few years ago exceeded 15% of GDP. They did this at enormous economic, social and political cost, and it is not a process that we recommend to those countries with a choice – which the non-Eurozone countries may not have had. Nonetheless, the speed of adjustment in the Eurozone countries has been quite slow. All of this is to illustrate how long and hard the road ahead is likely to be for the member states of the Eurozone. Faced with such a daunting path ahead, it is easy to anticipate that the European Union will be overwhelmingly preoccupied with its own internal difficulties for the foreseeable future – and that major new initiatives for global cooperation are likely to be low on the EU's list of priorities.

Figure 3.1 Changes in unit labour costs and the consumer price index, various Eurozone countries, 2007–2011

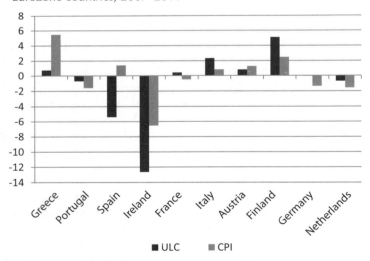

Source: G B Wolff, 'Why is Rebalancing in Europe so Painfully Slow?', Bruegel, 14 Mar 2012, at *http://www.bruegel.org/blog/detail/article/705-why-is-rebalancing-in-europe-so-painfully-slow* (accessed 4 Apr 2012); data from Eurostat .

Figure 3.2 Adjustment in Eurozone and non-Eurozone deficit countries, 2007–2011 (current account deficits as a percentage of GDP)

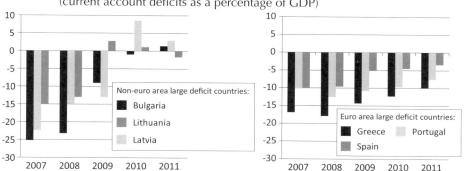

Source: Silvia Merler and Jean Pisani-Ferry, *Sudden Stops in the Euro Area*, Bruegel Policy Contribution Issue 2012/06, Mar 2012; data from ECFIN Forecasts, Nov 2011 .

3.5   The China syndrome

Confronting the imbalances outside Europe will be no less difficult. The global crisis has accelerated pressure on China to move away from the economic model it has pursued for some 30 years. We address longer-term issues below; for now, we observe that rapid Chinese growth has been driven by a panoply of measures that constrained growth in household income and consumption, pushed the Chinese savings rate up to levels that eventually exceeded even the country's very high investment rate, and stimulated production for export. There is widespread agreement that Chinese trade surpluses of the size that have prevailed over the past decade cannot be sustained – even if the Chinese wanted to sustain them, the appetite to absorb these surpluses in North America and Europe has waned.

In order to adjust to the new reality, the Chinese government will have to reverse a series of long-established policies with powerful supporters within China. For political reasons, the adjustment has had to be postponed until at least 2012 because of the leadership transition and the need to develop a consensus; but the longer the postponement, the more difficult the transition will be. Within China, debates on the urgency and nature of the economic transition, and on the distribution of the gains and losses associated with a reform of the current economic growth model, have become contentious. It remains unclear how the debate within China will resolve itself, which also leaves unclear what role China will play in cooperation with the international community to address the issues we identify in this paper.

While China's current account surplus has dropped since the crisis, this has been driven almost wholly by external conditions, as can be seen from the relationship between the savings and investment accounts. Key underpinnings of the surplus-generating model remain in place (of which more in Chapter 5 below). As Figure 3.3 indicates, the savings rate has substantially exceeded investment ever since 1994, when Beijing sharply devalued the renminbi. The resulting current account surpluses have been central to China's economic strategy, and they grew continually and dramatically over the course of the last decade.

Figure 3.3 China's saving and investment as share of GDP

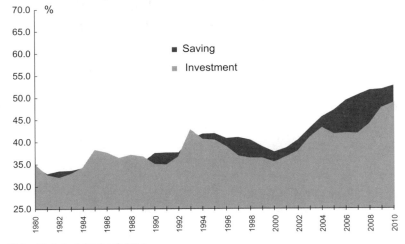

Source: China Statistical Yearbook 2011.

China could reduce these surpluses by decreasing savings, or increasing investment, or both. Beijing has consistently proclaimed its major economic policy objective to be, since at least 2007, to reduce savings by increasing domestic consumption, which has been severely constrained by a range of government policies. This would allow the Chinese people to realise more of the benefits of the country's economic success, and would reduce the country's reliance upon exports as the engine of economic growth. But the surplus can also be reduced by increasing investment without affecting savings, and this in fact is what has happened in the past several years.

The Chinese government responded to the Great Recession with a surge in investment after 2008. This may have been an appropriate policy response - otherwise growth would have collapsed – but in the absence of more fundamental changes, it will not be enough. For one thing, in order to stimulate increased investment the government has continued to hold borrowing rates extremely low, and to repress interest rates at the expense of household depositors; as a result, households have to increase their savings rates to make up the difference. So national savings continue to rise, and the surpluses are not reduced.

True adjustment would involve a substantial increase in domestic consumption, but consumption has not increased its share of GDP since the onset of the crisis. This is not surprising, as it would require a major reorientation of economic policy – with serious political and economic implications. Beijing has tried to increase the consumption share of GDP by subsidising certain types of household consumption (white goods, cars), but since the subsidies are paid for indirectly by the household sector, the net effect is to take away with one hand what it offers with the other.

Since 2005, when Beijing first announced its intention to reverse the declining consumption share of GDP, policymakers have found it very hard to raise the consumption rate. Inasmuch as consumption-constraining policies are central to the current growth model, this is unlikely to change quickly. However, there is talk about reducing the current very high investment rate, and during much of 2012 both credit growth and loan growth have fallen, in line with the stated intentions of policymakers. This implies that the current account surplus will persist at least above 4% of GDP in the next few years, as the prospects for a dramatic shift in Chinese policy seem slim. And yet it is not at all clear that the current international environment will permit China even to return to the level of current account surpluses it had run before the crisis began. In the absence of aggressive action to adjust to new conditions, China may face the possibility of much slower growth. What is more, a Chinese slowdown would be a serious adverse shock to developing countries heavily reliant on commodity exports.

3.6   Japan struggles back

Adjustment in both Europe and China is complicated by the difficulties Japan is facing in dealing with the aftermath of the very trying last 20 years. After the financial crisis of the early 1990s, over the course of one or two lost decades, government debt soared from roughly 20–30% of GDP in 1990 to 220% of GDP today. Tokyo is now planning to act to increase national savings by reducing government spending and investment; raising taxes, especially consumption taxes, beginning in 2014; and continuing to put downward pressure on wages and salaries, which have declined over the past decade. This was part of a broader process of forcing down overall wages relative to GDP in an effort to increase Japan's international competitiveness.

These may seem like reasonable steps for a country struggling to address a substantial government debt load, but they cannot help but have significantly adverse effects on global attempts to restore more balanced trade and capital movements. In other words, after 20 years in which Japan gradually recovered from the excesses of the 1980s – bringing down its extraordinarily high savings rate and its current account surplus – Japan is set to reverse course, constrain domestic consumption and push up its current account surplus.

The sense of urgency in Japan may have been exacerbated by recent reductions in the country's current account surplus, caused in part by reconstruction efforts related to the March 2011 earthquake and tsunami. In fact, in January 2012, Japan experienced, for only the fifth time on record and the first since January 2009, a monthly current account deficit. Since then the current account has swung back into surplus, but the lower surpluses overall have ignited concerns about Tokyo's ability to manage its rising debt burden. All of this is occurring just as the world urgently needs more consumption from low-consuming Asia.

3.7   Recovery, and then what?

In the aftermath of the Great Recession, in short, it is not clear that the underlying problems that led to the crisis have been adequately addressed. The major surplus regions of the world have largely returned to, continued or redoubled the policies that created the global imbalances that were central to the crisis itself. Figure 3.4 shows the pattern of current account balances among broadly defined regions of the world over the past 15 years, with IMF projections for the next five. The projections are in fact for current account surpluses to remain near the levels of the past decade.[9] Meanwhile, other weaknesses that contributed to the crisis – such as the apparent inability of financial regulators to keep up with the activities of modern globalised financial markets – continue to plague the world economy.

The lack of progress on macroeconomic policy coordination, in particular, seems to us a serious problem. Most of the debtor countries have been, or will be, forced to adjust by the realities of international financial markets, and by the unwillingness or inability of national publics to accept continued deficits. It is hard to imagine a return to an era in which large-scale current account deficits are counterbalanced by debt-financed consumption in the US and peripheral Europe. However, the surplus countries are not acting on their own to alter their relationship to the rest of the world economy (or, in the case of northern Europe, to the rest of the Eurozone). This suggests that, left to their own devices, national governments are likely to head towards a new round of macroeconomic imbalances, with the attendant risks of another round of major financial crises. Only sounder domestic economic policies supported by substantial internationally coordinated action can avoid a return to the brink of the abyss.

Figure 3.4 Global current account imbalances, as a percentage of world GDP

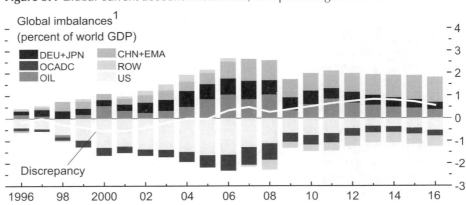

Notes: China + EMA: China, Hong Kong SAR, Indonesia, Korea, Malaysia, Philippines, Singapore, Taiwan Province of China and Thailand; DEU + JPN: Germany and Japan; OCADC: Bulgaria, Croatia, Czech Republic, Estonia, Greece, Hungary, Ireland, Latvia, Lithuania, Poland, Portugal, Romania, Slovak Republic, Slovenia, Spain, Turkey and UK; OIL: oil exporters; ROW: rest of world; US: United States.

Source: IMF, *World Economic Outlook*, Sept 2011. Figures for 2011– are IMF estimates.

---

9   Chinn *et al* (2011) presents a careful analysis that arrives at similar conclusions.

4 Global Economic Coordination: On Track or Doomed to Fail?

The Great Recession that began in 2007, and the global financial panic of late 2008, illustrated the importance of international cooperation in times of crisis. Today, we face the possibility that uncoordinated national policies, driven by national concerns for pressing domestic problems, will bring us back to the precarious conditions that made the Great Recession and the global financial panic possible. These are strong reasons to hope for a substantial increase in international economic cooperation among the major centres of economic activity. And yet the record of such cooperation is extremely spotty, even in the midst of the gravest economic crisis of the past 75 years.

4.1 Globalisation and governance

Contemporary globalisation, which has evolved progressively since the end of WWII, began to intensify markedly during the last decade of the past century. The fall of the Berlin Wall, the structural adjustment towards more openness in many developing countries, the conclusion of the Uruguay Round, the proliferation of regional trade agreements, the beginning of the emergence of China as a global economic power, and the information technology revolution are all associated with this intensification. By the second half of that decade, Michael Bordo, Barry Eichengreen and Doug Irwin (1999) were arguing that our globalisation had surpassed, at least on the trade and financial fronts, that phenomenon's previous great era 100 years earlier. At the same time, however, one of the authors of this report was asking whether globalisation had not already gone too far (Rodrik, 1997).

Bordo *et al* noted that it was surprising, given the degree of market integration, that trade tensions and financial crises had not become even more severe than they had been a century before. They hypothesised that the multilateral institutions built over the second half of the 20th century had provided a substitute – albeit an imperfect one – for global governance. At the end of their essay, they cautioned, however, that 'Governments seeking to make the world safe for global capitalism still have a ways to go' (1999, p 58).

The brute force of events, if nothing else, illustrated the accuracy of that statement. The sudden reversals in capital flows that occurred in Mexico (1994), East Asia (1997), Russia (1998), and later Brazil (1999) and Argentina (2001), shocked the international financial system and created awareness that the unprecedented degree of financial globalisation brought with it substantial risks. Even before those traumatic episodes, it seemed that the gap was growing rapidly between the evolution of markets, on the one hand, and governance structures, on the other, that could level the playing field, correct negative externalities, compensate for asymmetric information and provide public goods (domestic and international). The financial crises of the second half of the 1990s seemed to provide the stimulus to start closing that gap decisively.

4.2   G20 rising

By 1998 ministers of finance of the largest developed and developing economies spoke of reforming the international financial architecture and began to group themselves in a new forum, the Group of 20 (G20) financial and monetary authorities. The purported mission was to create an institutional framework that would prevent massive crises, or at least make it less difficult to manage them if they occurred, without depriving emerging countries of a sustained inflow of capital from their developed counterparts. Those years saw talk of bold initiatives, like making the International Monetary Fund a true international lender of last resort (Fischer, 1999; Krueger, 2001), amending the IMF Articles of Agreement to provide sovereign governments with bankruptcy-style protections, and changing significantly the IMF's voting structure. The United Nations Millennium Summit of September 2000 appeared as a catalytic event where the international community, while embracing globalisation as a positive force for prosperity, also made clear that success in realising the full effects of that force would depend on good governance within each country as well as at the international level (UN General Assembly, 2000).

In November 2001, in the midst of uncertain geopolitical circumstances in the aftermath of 9/11, countries strongly reaffirmed their commitment to the deepening of globalisation, launching the ninth round of multilateral trade liberalisations in Doha, Qatar. Also at that meeting, after negotiations of almost 15 years, the accession of China to the World Trade Organization was at last approved.

4.3   Momentum unsustained

The multilateral momentum seemed to continue with the adoption of the Monterrey Consensus in March 2002. The Consensus, in addition to providing an unprecedented commitment of international financial cooperation for development, endorsed concrete steps to enhance the coherence, governance and consistency of the international monetary, financial and trading systems (Monterrey Consensus, 2003). The document, which was endorsed by the large number of leaders of developed and developing countries attending the conference, speaks of the importance of continuing to improve global economic governance, of strong coordination of macroeconomic policies, of the need for the IMF to strengthen its surveillance activities over all economies, of the need to ensure that the IMF has a suitable array of financial facilities and resources to respond to financial crises, and of strengthening international tax cooperation. It now looks remarkable that it was in large part the driving force of the US that pushed forward the Monterrey Consensus and the launching of the Doha Round, inasmuch as that government would soon earn the reputation for being one of the most unilateralist US Administrations in recent history.

However, the ambitious aspirations for reform and international cooperation went unrealised. Apart from some enlargement and flexibilisation of the IMF's financing capacity, no new international financial architecture was ever really built. The Doha Development Round, whose negotiations were supposed to conclude no later than 1 January 2005, has become one of the most disappointing undertakings in the history of the multilateral trading system. Failure to compromise and agree on the issues included in the Doha agenda led to repeated collapses of the negotiations between September 2003 and August 2008.

4.4 Problems proliferate

While governments were failing to fulfil their commitments for stronger international coordination, the need for it was increasing. After the modest slowdown of the world economy in 2001/2, the pace of globalisation accelerated and changes in the structure of the world economy that had started earlier on became quickly accentuated.

Computing and telecommunication capabilities became cheaper and more powerful, which made it increasingly attractive to decompose previously integrated and concentrated production processes and to form internationalised supply chains that became highly competitive. As Richard Baldwin (2011) has put it, what used to be about economies of scale, vertical integration and production clusters is now about fragmenting productive processes and finding the most profitable location for each fragment. Each good or service sold at the end of its supply chain is a conjunction of many countries' capital, labour, technology, infrastructure, finance and business environments. This new organisation of production is having far-reaching implications for the international division of labour, and is changing the global pattern of production and trade probably faster than ever in history.

One consequence is that developing countries do not need to wait until they have sufficient large-scale industries to achieve fast industrialisation. In fact, they do not even have to build supply chains; they just have to join them competitively in order to speed their industrialisation. Another consequence is that countries' comparative advantage is no longer about finished goods or commodities; it is about the finer tasks that make up the manufacturing, commercial and financial processes necessary to ultimately produce and deliver the goods demanded by consumers (Grossman and Rossi-Hansberg, 2006). It also follows that less and less international trade is a flow between two locations – goods produced in one country sold to customers in another – and more and more is becoming a web of multidirectional flows connecting numerous locations.

No developing country has taken better advantage of the new organisation of production and trade than China. Thanks to its quick assimilation into global supply chains and rapidly expanding participation in the flows of global trade, China's economic growth has accelerated dramatically over the last quarter of a century. In the process, China has become a country with an immense trade surplus. It is not only the second largest destination for FDI, but at the same time one of the largest global investors, and certainly the holder of the largest foreign exchange reserves, in the world. Although not as spectacularly as China, over the same period other developing countries – not least India, the other Asian giant – also emerged as important players in the world economy, thanks to faster economic growth. Consequently, for more than two decades the developing economies have grown faster than the developed ones; this is translating into a markedly different distribution of global GDP. The developed countries, which had kept a share of global output of around 60% from 1950 to 1990, have now seen that share reduced to less than 50% (Maddison, 2010; Buiter and Rahbari, 2011).

If the abrupt reversal of capital flows from rich to emerging countries was seen as a chief risk to the stability of the international financial system during the last two decades of the 20th century, the story had changed dramatically by the middle of the first decade of this century. By virtue of very high domestic savings that translated into huge current account surpluses, fast growing emerging economies, particularly China, became massive financiers of rich countries' large current account deficits, particularly that of the US.[10]

4.5   Warnings issued

By 2006 the global imbalances had become a serious cause of concern for many analysts of the global economy, although others, including some distinguished members of the economics profession, were providing rather benign tales about the causes and consequences of those imbalances.[11] To its credit, the IMF's management took the global imbalances seriously, not only by extending repeated warnings in the institution's basic reports, but also by eventually making members agree on a process of multilateral consultation on global imbalances, which was announced in April of 2006 (IMF, 2006a). The IMF carried out its consultation on global imbalances, focusing tactfully on the US, China, the Eurozone, Japan and Saudi Arabia, then presented its report in April 2007. The report was expeditiously ignored or dismissed precisely by those who had given the institution the go-ahead for the consultation.

Ironically, the IMF was still licking its wounds from both the rebuttal by its key members of the multilateral consultation exercise and a mandate to reduce drastically its personnel and other operating expenses while adapting to a new

---

10   Of course, rich countries like Germany and Japan contributed to the unprecedented savings surplus.
11   Zedillo (2006); Bernanke (2005); Cooper (2005); Hausmann and Sturzenegger (2006).

managing director – the third in less than five years – when the international financial system started to crack with the eruption of the sub-prime crisis in the late summer of 2007. Although some of the root causes of the crisis could be traced to strictly domestic policy decisions in the countries where it erupted, ultimately the crisis happened because the key players in the global economy failed to address, in a coordinated way, significant issues stemming from the intensification of globalisation, despite the fact that those issues had been identified early on as threats to international financial stability.

4.6 Warnings heeded?

Considering that lack of adequate collective action was a chief cause of the crisis, the formation of the G20 was excellent news, despite the dramatic circumstances that triggered it in the fall of 2008. It seemed that at last the leaders of the largest economies in the world would take up the challenge of filling the governance gap. It was encouraging to learn that at their first summit meeting in November 2008, the G20 leaders themselves admitted that inconsistent and insufficiently coordinated policies had led to the crisis, and that on this occasion and at two subsequent meetings, they made concrete commitments to bring about that purported cooperation (G20, 2008b, para 3).

During its first three summits, the attention of the G20 focused largely on reform of financial systems, preservation of open markets, reinforcement of the multilateral financial institutions and, of course, macroeconomic policy coordination.

Not surprisingly, given how the crisis erupted, the G20 gave much attention to issues of their financial sectors. At their first summit, the G20 leaders bluntly identified 'weak underwriting standards, unsound risk management practices, increasingly complex and opaque financial products, and consequent excessive leverage' as root causes of the crisis. They frankly charged that 'policy makers, regulators and supervisors, in some advanced countries, did not adequately appreciate and address the risks building up in financial markets, keep pace with financial innovation, or take into account the systemic ramifications of domestic regulatory actions' (G20, 2008b, para 3). Although stressing that regulation is first and foremost a national responsibility, and agreeing on a set of common principles to exercise that responsibility, the G20 was equally emphatic in claiming that the increasing globalism of financial markets needed intensified international cooperation in order to mitigate adverse cross-border externalities stemming from those markets.

The G20's apprehension about the multiple weak flanks of financial markets was expressed in a long list of commitments articulated both in their Washington and London declarations. In a noticeable display of granularity for a leaders' summit, the G20 at Washington committed to immediate and medium-term actions aimed at reinforcing regulation, transparency, accountability, integrity and prudential oversight of financial markets. The G20's to-do list at that meeting hardly left any aspect of financial markets untouched. It was not an exaggeration to present it as a 'comprehensive work plan' for reform. Accounting standards, credit rating agencies, unregulated instruments and markets, credit default swaps and over-the-counter derivatives, compensation schemes, investor and consumer protection, capital requirements, and resolution regimes and bankruptcy laws, plus a few others, were issues purported to be to be dealt with diligently by the G20 membership. It looked as if the G20 was providing a common platform for a coordinated move towards sweeping reform in all the members' financial systems. In every section of the G20's Washington work plan for financial reform, the importance of international cooperation is duly stressed. The boldness of the language used should have left no room for doubt:

> We call upon our national and regional regulators to formulate their regulations and other measures in a consistent manner. Regulators should enhance their coordination and cooperation across all segments of financial markets, including with respect to cross-border capital flows. Regulators and other relevant authorities as a matter of priority should strengthen cooperation on crisis prevention, management, and resolution. (G20, 2008b, para 9)

The emphasis on fixing the financial system and the role of cross-border coordination did not diminish at the second summit of April 2009. The Action Plan adopted at the first meeting was not only re-endorsed but also reinforced with some additional decisions, such as the elevation of the Financial Stability Forum to Board status – by virtue of expanded membership and additional responsibilities – and an agreement on the basic criteria for what eventually would become the third Basel Accord.

4.7   Warnings forgotten

The sense of urgency for undertaking financial reform under the terms stipulated at Washington and London was clearly diminished by the time of the third summit in the fall of 2009. At Pittsburgh, the G20 claimed to have developed 'sweeping reforms' and to have achieved 'substantial progress' in strengthening prudential oversight and transparency, improving risk management, promoting market integrity and reinforcing international cooperation, none of which was by then in fact the case (G20, 2009a, para 11). Admittedly, that summit did produce an additional push for new capital and liquidity requirements, as well as some commitments on the intended timing for reforms on compensation, trading and clearing of OTC derivatives, global accounting standards, and prudential standards of systemically important financial institutions.

Some of those deadlines – like completing implementation of the work in progress on new capital and liquidity standards – were reiterated at the fourth Toronto summit, but the sense of urgency for financial sector reform continued to decrease, perhaps due to a combination of complacency stemming from the early signs of recovery, and realism about the difficulty of undertaking the actions agreed early on. The tone of urgency continued to fade at the Seoul meeting of November 2010. Although the Basel III Accord that had been released in September of 2010 was endorsed and none of the other significant issues were ignored in the G20's declaration, the level of precision about most commitments was clearly subdued. By contrast, one topic of financial reform that was meriting increasing attention was that of the systemically important financial institutions (SIFIs), where dealing with cross-border recovery and resolution questions is clearly unavoidable.

That attention was kept at the following G20 Summit at Cannes in November 2011, where the work of the Financial Stability Board (FSB) for a comprehensive policy framework on the topic, including its determination of which banks should be considered globally systemically important, was endorsed. Another topic that received special attention at Cannes, because of its potential for creating regulatory arbitrage and systemic risk, was that of the shadow banking system, whose regulation and oversight the G20 agreed to strengthen.

In any case, by the Seoul meeting the pledges for international coordination of financial reforms so prominent at the first two summits had diminished significantly, if not disappeared altogether. The benign explanation is that it was no longer necessary to insist on this emphasis, given the institutionalisation of coordination already achieved through the FSB and other organisations. More likely, the lesser emphasis on coordination was recognition that, contrary to the early pledges, some of the major players had proceeded unilaterally with their respective reform undertakings. The US Dodd-Frank Financial Reform is a case in point, but not the only one. Other jurisdictions have put in place laws or regulations without ensuring that they are – as originally offered – collectively consistent. When notice is taken of conflicts that are arising as a result of norms such as the 'Volcker Rule', OTC derivatives, shadow banks and even capital requirements, it is tempting to say that the G20 substantially gave up its early pledge of coordination around 2010.

4.8   Trade failing

The same can also be said about some of the G20's key commitments on trade. At Washington, the G20 gave a commitment to 'refrain from raising new barriers to investment or to trade in goods and services, imposing new export restrictions, or implementing World Trade Organization (WTO) inconsistent measures to stimulate exports' (G20, 2008b, para 13). It also pledged to put the Doha Round back on track towards a successful conclusion. At London, these commitments were reiterated, as they were also at Pittsburgh, with an important addition. At the latter summit, the G20 leaders declared that they were 'determined to seek an ambitious and balanced conclusion to the Doha Development Round in 2010' (G20, 2009a, para 49). It is interesting to notice that while in London they committed to reach a conclusion of the Round, acknowledging that it was urgently needed. At Pittsburgh, they committed not to 'reach', but to 'seek' that conclusion, sweetening the downgrade with the 2010 deadline.

That deadline was dropped altogether by the following summit in Toronto, although the commitment to promptly bring the round to conclusion was preserved all the way up to the Seoul summit. By the time of the Cannes meeting, the sense of failure was inescapable. Laconically the G20 declared, 'We stand by the Doha Development Agenda (DDA) mandate. However, it is clear that we will not complete the DDA if we continue to conduct negotiations as we have in the past. We recognise the progress achieved so far' (G20, 2011c, para 66).

4.9   IFI reform on the agenda

Naturally, under the impulse of the crisis, the G20 immediately went back to the old, but repeatedly unfulfilled, objective of reforming the international financial institutions (IFIs). Right from the start, at the first summit of November 2008, they set as a short-term objective to look at the adequacy of those institutions' resources. Maybe remorseful about the mistreatment applied to the IMF with its multilateral surveillance exercise of the previous year, the G20 stated: 'The IMF should conduct vigorous and even-handed surveillance reviews of all countries, as well as giving greater attention to their financial sectors and better integrating the reviews with the joint IMF/World Bank financial assessment programs' – although this was qualified as a medium term objective. Also sounding remorseful, the G20 'underscored that the Bretton Woods Institutions must be comprehensively reformed so that they can more adequately reflect changing economic weights in the world economy and be more responsive to future challenges' (G20, 2008a).

More boldly, at the G20 London summit, the leaders admitted that they had to strengthen the World Bank's and – more importantly given the circumstances of the day – the IMF's relevance, effectiveness and legitimacy. The G20 leaders literally affirmed that they would reform those institutions' mandates, scope and governance to reflect changes in the world economy and the new challenges of globalisation, and – as they had said at Washington – would give emerging countries greater voice and representation. Pertinently, and complying with their earlier commitment, they also agreed upon the allocation of significantly larger resources to the IMF, a decision that allowed the institution to help put out fires before they spread in some emerging countries that came under financial stress.

The attention given by the G20 to the IMF at the Pittsburgh summit had two somewhat contradictory components. One was in the direction of strengthening the institution by stating that the modernisation of the IMF's governance was essential to improve its credibility, legitimacy and effectiveness, and backing this statement with a commitment to address – as part of a quota review process to be concluded by early 2011 – issues such as size and composition of the Executive Board, enhancement of the Board's effectiveness, and involvement by the Fund Governors in its strategic oversight (G20, 2009a, para 21). At the same time, the IMF's authority to exercise its surveillance responsibility was clearly diminished when the G20, in order to deal with the correction of the global macroeconomic imbalances, opted for a sort of peer review mechanism (titled Mutual Assessment Process, or MAP) in which the IMF was assigned an essentially subsidiary role of just giving technical assistance to the G20's finance ministers and central bank governors (G20, 2009a, para 7).

Some, but not all, of the committed reforms in the IMF's representation and governance had been agreed by the time of the G20 Seoul meeting in November 2010. A shift in quota share, mostly in favour of the largest emerging economies, and an offer to reflect that shift in the institution's executive board – reforms that fell quite short of changing the balance of power among the members in any significant way – was the step taken and it was underlined as an important one at that summit.[12] Possibly more consequential was the G20's call for the IMF to play a bigger role in the MAP (G20, 2010, para 11) and to relaunch its earlier commitment to enhance the IMF's surveillance mandate and action (G20, 2010, para 20).

The IMF's repositioning on the G20's radar was undoubtedly caused by the lacklustre evolution of the MAP since its launch in September 2009 and up to the meeting in Seoul. It should have been clear by then not only that the MAP was moving very slowly, but that despite early pledges, the structural correction of the global macroeconomic imbalances was still pending; furthermore the very serious debt problem of several members of the European monetary union was evident. At that point and at subsequent events throughout 2011, the diagnosis provided by the G20 at its first summit about what caused the crisis in the first place should have resonated loudly: 'Major underlying factors to the current situation were, among others, inconsistent and insufficiently coordinated macroeconomic policies, inadequate structural reforms, which led to unsustainable global macroeconomic outcomes. These developments, together, contributed to excesses and ultimately resulted in severe market disruption' (G20, 2008b, para 4).

Although at the G20 Pittsburgh meeting of September 2009, the language to stress the importance of the global imbalances was subdued relative to that used in the Washington communiqué, it is clear that the imbalances continued to be a central concern of leaders (G20, 2009a). So much so that they launched the above-mentioned MAP with the goal, among others, to 'ensure that fiscal, monetary, trade and structural policies are collectively consistent with more sustainable and balanced trajectories of growth', and also to collectively 'undertake macro prudential and regulatory policies to help prevent credit and asset price cycles from becoming forces of destabilization' (G20, 2009a). This statement of purpose was impeccable; however, the G20, rather than empowering the IMF to perform its multilateral surveillance duty, adopted 'a cooperative process of mutual assessment' where members themselves would agree on shared policy objectives, set medium-term policy frameworks, assess the collective implications of national policies and identify risks to financial stability. How this sort of peer review mechanism would in fact work was left to be agreed later by the G20 ministers.

Ministers did provide, at St Andrews in Scotland, not long after the Pittsburgh meeting, a timetable for developing the mutual assessment process (G20, 2009b). According to that timetable, each country would provide its own

---

12   For a brief description of the reforms agreed in November 2010, see IMF (2010).

policy framework and projections by end of January 2010. With this input, the G20 – supported by the IMF and the World Bank – would conduct the initial phase of the MAP, checking the consistency of national policies with the collective objectives, and develop accordingly a basket of policy options for leaders to consider at the June 2010 Toronto Summit. Ultimately the objective, supposedly after refining the MAP, was to present leaders with more specific policy recommendations for their decision at their Seoul Summit of November 2010.

4.10 Multilateral surveillance frustrated

That the MAP as depicted at Pittsburgh would prove to be ineffectual was confirmed by the fact that the deadlines agreed by the G20 ministers at St Andrews were not effectively met. There was no basket of policy options ready for Toronto, nor more specific recommendations ready for Seoul, where, instead, leaders settled for a call to their subordinates to develop 'indicative guidelines composed of a range of indicators' that 'would serve as a mechanism to facilitate timely identification of large imbalances that require preventive and corrective actions to be taken' (G20, 2010, para 11).[13]

Only at their February 2011 meeting in Paris were finance ministers able to agree on three types of indicators to assess national economic policies. These indicators are public debts and fiscal deficits, private savings rates and private debts, and external imbalances composed of the trade balance and net investment income flows and transfers, with exchange rate, fiscal, monetary and other policies being left to be taken only into 'due consideration' (G20, 2011a, para 3).

It took the G20 ministers one more meeting to agree on four approaches (one 'structural' and three 'statistical') to determine the guidelines against which the previously determined indicators would be assessed. Ministers also agreed that countries identified as having persistently large imbalances by at least two of the approaches would be further assessed 'to determine in a second step the nature and root causes of their imbalances and impediments to adjustment' (G20, 2011b). Although asking the IMF to carry out the task of applying the indicators and approaches agreed by the ministers to identify the problematic cases did devolve some technical authority to the institution, it is also clear that a peculiar mix of over-prescription and ambiguity limited such devolution.

The IMF has tried to do its best to exercise its rather limited technical mandate by producing and making public a set of staff reports for the G20 MAP (IMF, 2011). The set consists of umbrella, accountability, MAP as well as individual sustainability reports for countries, which given the relative size of their economies and their imbalances are considered to have the greater potential for spillover effects (US, China, Japan, India, Germany, UK and France).

---

13   It is interesting to notice that the failure to deliver at Seoul what was committed at Pittsburgh and at St Andrews has been, after the fact, presented as if the first stage of the MAP, consisting of two steps, had actually been achieved. See IMF Factsheet (IMF, 2012).

Although it is hard to know exactly how much influence the IMF MAP reports might have had in the preparation of the G20 documents released at the Cannes Summit, it seems that the G20 Action Plan for Growth and Jobs agreed there, as well as the one adopted at the Los Cabos Summit of June 2012, have been heavily influenced by the IMF's own analyses and assessments. It is yet to be seen whether and how these modest steps could signal a trend where the centre of gravity of the G20 MAP moves away from the ineffectual peer review mechanism originally intended and towards the IMF's independent analysis.

4.11 Promises, promises…

Admittedly, it is too soon to pass definitive judgement on the G20's performance as an effective catalyst of international collective action. It is true that some key decisions taken during the initial phases of the crisis that erupted in the fall of 2008 – such as the adoption of fiscal stimulus and monetary easing to prevent a total collapse of aggregate demand, the commitment to avoid an explosion of protectionism and the announcement of additional resources for the IMF – have come to be associated with the G20. But it is also true that it could be argued that the various fiscal stimulus packages implemented in 2009 could have happened anyway, as it is similarly true that the extremely useful coordination among monetary authorities since the summer of 2007 is rooted in a long-standing practice of communication and collaboration among central bankers.[14] It is less clear that the commitments to avoid protectionism and give the IMF more ammunition would have been taken so early in the absence of the G20.

It is certain, however, that the G20 is still far from earning its self-designated stature of 'premier forum for international cooperation' (G20, 2009a, para 19), as proven by its rather limited efficacy to deal with the key issues on the agenda of its own making. Passing that test of efficacy is essential to provide the G20 with much needed legitimacy. Being a group of self-appointed members, albeit producing altogether more than 80% of global GDP, the G20's origin has weak political legitimacy. This shortcoming will only be circumvented if it shows to the international community – and certainly to each member's national constituencies – that it can take and execute important decisions that make a positive difference for each G20 country and the world at large.

The chances of achieving such efficacy and legitimacy have been eroded by the G20's failure to deliver fully on a number of important commitments contained in the four key avenues for action established by the group itself in its first two meetings – financial reform, open markets, IFIs and macroeconomic policy coordination. The G20 has compounded its credibility problem by introducing other issues into its agenda, but not solving them. Pledges on reduction of poverty, infrastructure, food security, energy security, climate change, marine environment and anti-corruption are examples of challenges that have crept into the G20's declarations and action plans.

---

14   In addition to their meetings at the IMF/World Bank Spring and Fall annual meetings, the Central Bank governors periodically get together at the Bank for International Settlements.

4.12 Failure explained, but not excused

If it is accepted that the world needs something like the G20, then it is important to enquire why this initiative so far has failed to live up to its initial promise. There is, of course, the circumstance that much of what the G20 has offered to deliver constitutes a global public good.[15] The need for collective action stems precisely from the nature of the G20's deliverables. Global financial stability and a rules-based multilateral non-discriminatory trading system – two of the basic endeavours of the G20 – are for the most part global public goods because, once provided, they can be enjoyed in principle by each country without impinging on the enjoyment of others. The objectives of financial stability and preventing trade protectionism are conceivably widely shared, but this does not mean that every state would be willing to put in its own share of effort to achieve them.

It is in the nature of global public goods that if left freely to the actions of the political and economic markets, their supply will tend to fall short of their demand. On the one hand, governments do not want to limit their sovereignty (or are politically constrained from doing so) by accepting binding rules and mechanisms to enforce their compliance. There is also the free-rider problem, which means that given the non-excludability of a public good, there is the incentive for each country to wait for others to provide it without sharing in the effort to supply it. The fact that many countries value public goods differently is also an obstacle to assembling the necessary collective action for the provision of global public goods. This circumstance is exacerbated now that countries that are still developing, and are even relatively poor, have become global economic powers due to the sheer size of their GDP and degree of engagement in the world economy.

It is mainly for these reasons that historically it has taken a special catalytic force to harness the international cooperation necessary to provide global public goods, a force that this time was supposed to be generated by the G20 and, more specifically, by some of its key members exercising enlightened leadership. Admittedly, even if a true wish to provide that leadership were present, as seemed to be the case at inception, in its initial steps the G20 member governments were bound to confront significant domestic political economy limitations in their ability to pursue the necessary international cooperation. As one of us warned early on in the crisis: 'There will be a natural tendency for economies and people to turn inward, and for governments to reduce the priority they give to their external ties. As they do so, there is a risk that they will slip toward a breakdown in international cooperation, and even toward conflict' (Frieden, 2009).

The concern underlying this prediction was that, once the emergency phase of the crisis was overcome, and as governments tried to pursue the adjustments and reforms needed to address the policy failures that caused the crisis, as well as the political factors that led to those failures, forces pulling away from internationally cooperative solutions would be unleashed to the point that governments would minimise or ignore the importance of fulfilling their commitment to cooperate.

---

15 For a discussion of global public goods please see International Task Force on Global Public Goods (2006). Ernesto Zedillo served as co-chair of the Task Force.

Since adjustment is never painless, even for surplus economies, in each country domestic politics would push towards shifting the burden of rebalancing to those foreign counterparts involved in the disequilibrium to be corrected, and away from the needed domestic effort. This circumstance reinforces the inherent political difficulty faced by governments in the construction of global public goods such as those entertained in the G20 agenda.

There is a profound disconnect between the G20's statement of purpose as laid out in their initial meetings and what has happened with economic policy in the US and in the European Union. This points towards what may be a deeper obstacle to the construction of the global public goods that are indispensable for globalisation's sustainability: the limitations of each domestic political system, democratic or not, to internalise the consequences of others' policies on their own economic performance, as well as the ramifications of their policies on others' performance.

5 The Domestic Political Economy of International Economic Cooperation

It is easy for observers to point out the desirability of all manner of international cooperative ventures and to bemoan the paucity of successful efforts in this direction. But policymakers – the ones who actually need to undertake the cooperation – face limits on their actions. They have to answer to domestic constituents, for a policymaker who ignores what his constituents want will not be a policymaker for very long. This is true in all political systems, inasmuch as they all have some social choice mechanism that determines who influences policy and politics – from a tiny elite to the broad electorate.

Governments will only make the sacrifices necessary to carry through on their international obligations if they have domestic support for these sacrifices. And constituents will only put up with costly and difficult measures if they are convinced that the benefits – in particular, the benefits of sustaining the country's international economic commitments – outweigh the not inconsequential costs. If we are to have a clear sense of the prospects for international economic cooperation, then, we need a clear sense of the domestic political constraints under which policymakers are likely to operate. It is to this that we now turn, concentrating on some of the main centres of economic influence: the US, the European Union, China and Brazil. These are not meant to reflect an exhaustive survey of the world's major powers, but rather to give a flavour of the kinds of domestic political obstacles that can stand in the way of well-laid plans for international cooperation (we consider that the European Union's problems are roughly analogous to other countries' 'domestic' concerns). The broad conclusion to which we are driven is that, in virtually all cases, the political incentives are heavily weighted on the side of focusing on domestic problems, even at the expense of international ones.[16]

---

16 Simmons (1997) demonstrates the impact of such social and political instability on cooperative efforts in the interwar period – to devastating effect.

5.1   The United States

While the US has weathered the crisis that began there in 2007, it faces some serious economic and social challenges. The underlying social and economic realities that were, in one way or another, at the root of the crisis persist, and have not been addressed by the country's political system.

Most immediately, US citizens have not fully undertaken the adjustments necessary to address the overhang of debt that continues to hamper recovery. While households have reduced consumption and increased saving, they have not done so in anything like the measure necessary to restore some balance to their finances. Creditors, in particular major financial institutions, are still struggling to adjust their balance sheets to allow a resumption of normal lending. It will undoubtedly be several years before we see the US financial system playing its appropriate role as intermediary between savers and investors. On other dimensions as well – such as the trade balance and post-crisis fiscal policy – basic adjustments have yet to be undertaken. We are confident that they will be eventually, and that by 2020 we will be firmly in a post-crisis environment.

Turning to the longer term, nonetheless, it seems clear that the US will face important choices. We assume that the country will not return to running current account deficits in the range of 5–7% of GDP. The reserve currency role of the dollar, and the safe haven role of the US, probably allows current account deficits of 2% of GDP, but more than that is unlikely – and probably also both unnecessary and unwise. But a 'rebalancing' in the US will require constraining consumption and raising savings. Inasmuch as it also requires increasing productivity, this requires turning around the relatively sluggish productivity growth of the past decade. After very rapid increases in labour productivity starting in the middle 1990s, largely associated with high-technology industries and the application of their technologies in other areas, productivity growth has slowed.

The US has almost certainly been underinvesting in human capital formation, especially in maths, science and other areas related to modern information technologies. It has also cut back its spending on research and development, so that Americans are now surpassed by foreign innovators in applications for *US* patents. Indeed, foreign patent applications have risen continually from about one-quarter of the total in the 1960s, to 44% in 2000, to over 50% today (US Patent Office, 2012). While this is not in itself worrisome – foreigners apply for US patents in part because of the nation's technological edge – the relative slowdown of Americans' applications is an indication of the country's more general slowdown in education and innovation in areas associated with maths, science and information technologies.

It is easy to identify important areas in which substantial investment, largely public, is desirable and may even be necessary. This includes the country's educational system and its economic infrastructure. However, it is equally easy to identify powerful pressures on the fiscal stance of the Federal government. In particular, the financing of Medicare and Social Security programmes require attention. The latter could be addressed with modest reforms – fully taxing benefits, raising the retirement age, reducing benefits and raising taxes by fairly small amounts. The former, however, is tightly tied up with the galloping increase in the cost of medical care, a problem for which the diagnosis, let alone the prescription, is very uncertain.

Americans face serious questions about the appropriate role of the Federal government, and of its financing. Whatever the country decides about the services it wants from the government – the level of national defence, the size and generosity of the social safety net, the extent of support for the elderly – it will need to pay for them and cannot continue indefinitely to borrow to finance them. However, there are major disagreements among Americans as to how these constraints should be met – by cutting back on spending, or increasing taxes, or some combination. These disagreements are fuelled by material differences within American society. The US has become substantially more unequal since the early 1970s, and the experience of the recent crisis has reinforced the socio-economic diversity – some income groups, and some regions, were extremely hard hit, while others were much less severely affected. The disagreements over the future course of US economic policy are also fuelled by serious partisan disagreements, motivated by both ideology and electoral politics.

US politics is likely to remain at least as divided, even as polarised, as it has become in the past decade. This means that the US is likely to be absorbed in its own battles, too much so to pay sufficient attention to conditions in the rest of the world or to how US policy might ameliorate global problems. The US will continue to want to exercise international economic leadership, but its ability to find the political consensus, and the resources, necessary to do so will be severely constrained.

The ability of the US to provide purposive international economic leadership will be hampered by the distractions of its difficult domestic political disputes. While major players in the US economy remain firmly committed to global engagement – foremost among them the country's internationally oriented financial institutions and corporations – there are other powerful interest groups that are unenthusiastic about further international economic commitments. Perhaps even more disturbing is the rapidly growing scepticism about the world economy on the part of 'Main Street' America. Public opinion towards globalisation has become increasingly negative, so that US citizens are now the most hostile to international trade of the 47 countries regularly surveyed by the Pew Charitable Trust (Pew Global Attitudes Project, 2007). Table 5.1, which shows American views towards agreements to liberalise trade, indicates that, by enormous majorities, Americans believe that freer trade costs the country jobs, reduces wages and slows the economy.

Socio-economic trends in the US threaten to deepen scepticism about the international economy. Attitudes towards globalisation tend to track income relatively closely. Table 5.2 illustrates the relationship: only those US citizens with household incomes above $100,000 a year hold positive views about trade liberalisation. Table 5.3 demonstrates the impact in one specific instance: only those Americans with some college education are favourably inclined towards trade with China. In this context, the deterioration of the country's income distribution has almost certainly fed sentiment hostile to or sceptical about globalisation.

Table 5.1 Most say trade agreements lead to job losses (percentage responding in each category)

Impact of free trade agreements on...

	Total %	Republican %	Democrat %	Independent %
Jobs in US				
Create jobs	9	6	14	7
Lead to job losses	64	67	55	69
No difference	27	27	31	24
Wages in US				
Make wages higher	9	6	13	9
Make wager lower	52	52	49	53
No difference	39	42	38	38
Nation's economy				
Lead to growth	22	20	27	19
Slow economy	50	55	42	53
No difference	28	25	31	28

Source: 'Americans Are of Two Minds on Trade', Pew Research Center for the People and the Press, 9 Nov 2010. Available at *http://pewresearch.org/pubs/1795/poll-free-trade-agreements-jobs-wages-economic-growth-china-japan-canada* (accessed 26 Mar 2012).

Table 5.2 Few say they have been helped financially by trade agreements (percentage responding in each category)

Impact of free trade agreements on personal finances:

	Helped %	Hurt %
Total	36	64
Education		
College grad+	46	54
Some college	36	64
HS or less	31	69
Family income		
$100,000 or more	52	48
$75-99,999	32	68
$30-74,999	30	70
Less than $30,000	33	67

Source: As Table 5.1.

Partisan effects are also worrisome for those who favour international economic integration. Tables 5.1 and 5.3 both point to the fact that Republicans are substantially more hostile to international trade than are Democrats. The very existence of a partisan difference of this sort – and to some extent it does not matter what the direction is – means that it is too politically dangerous for US politicians to express open support for globalisation or its component parts.

Table 5.3 Views of increased trade with China (percentage responding in each category)

	Good for U.S. %	Bad for U.S. %
Total	50	50
By party		
Republican	45	55
Democrat	53	47
Independent	51	49
By education		
College grad+	56	44
Some college	54	46
HS or less	43	57

Source: As Table 5.1.

US policymakers and Americans more generally, are likely to be even more wary of foreign economic entanglements than they have been in the past. It seems that, at best, average Americans will be generally indifferent to what goes on in the rest of the world economy; at worst, they may be openly hostile.

5.2   The European Union

The ongoing crisis in the Eurozone is only one indication of how serious are the internal challenges facing the member states of the European Union. In a broad historical sense, the EU is an extraordinary success, as it has created the largest single market in world history, and the largest multinational economic union. At least until recently, even the euro could reasonably be regarded as a general success.

Nonetheless, the EU confronts some major concerns and, considering the EU as an economic entity, these internal problems are likely to absorb most of its energies for the foreseeable future. Most immediately, it has to avoid the collapse of the monetary union. Next, the member states will have to make the euro politically and economically sustainable by addressing several difficult issues, none of which has yet been settled. The first is the application of a common monetary policy to countries with divergent economic structures. The second is the absence of any meaningful coordination of fiscal policies. The third is the creation of a common financial system with disparate (national) financial regulators and regulations. The fourth is the lack of an explicit lender of last resort function on the part of the common central bank. The final problem is the existence of an implicit expectation that Eurozone member states will bail out Eurozone countries in crisis, which leads to serious problems of moral hazard.

Members of the Eurozone will have to work out its inherent weaknesses even as it gradually expands to include more EU member states. For it will be very difficult to exclude central and eastern European countries that have already starting asking for inclusion in the Eurozone. However, the incorporation of still more relatively poor nations, with economic structures even more different from those of the core Eurozone countries, raises the spectre of a return to the intra-Eurozone macroeconomic imbalances that were at the root of the Eurozone crisis. The EU will have, then, to repair the structure of the Eurozone as currently constituted, but it will have to do so as the Eurozone becomes a moving target, with more countries joining.

The European Union more broadly will have to deal with its internal structure. It is still very much open for debate whether the EU will be able to sustain the two-track organisation that has emerged. While the principle of subsidiarity is well established, it was never really meant to generate a union with two groups of countries moving in very different directions. The UK and other non-euro member states – including, most likely, some important central and eastern European ones such as Poland and the Czech Republic – seem headed in the direction of something close to associate membership in the much more closely integrated core Eurozone. This may be tenable; but it may also give rise to internal tensions that will erupt into major intra-European conflicts over the future of the European Union.

All this is on top of the inherent economic problems that the member states of the EU face, even without having to worry about the structure of the union itself. Demographic trends in Europe are even more troubling than in the US. The old-age dependency ratio for the EU-25, already at 25 in 2005, is expected to reach 32 by 2020 and to exceed 40 by 2030 (the old-age dependency ratio is the ratio of people 65 and over to those between 15 and 64, multiplied by 100). This means that while there are currently four working-age Europeans for every European 65 and over, in less than 20 years there will be only 2.5 working-age Europeans per elderly person. This is likely to put an unsustainable burden on pensions, and more generally on government finances.

As in the US, public opinion in Europe has become quite a bit more unfavourable towards international economic integration. Table 5.4 compares opinions on trade in France to those in the US and China. While most people in all three countries think trade is good for the economy, national companies and consumers, the French are firmly convinced that trade is bad for job creation, job security and the environment. More broadly within the European Union, Table 5.5 explores public opinion on international economic integration and cooperation. While attitudes towards globalisation in general remain positive – albeit less so in France than elsewhere – Europeans overwhelmingly believe that globalisation makes society more unequal, and that it is only good for large companies, not for people like them. When asked explicitly about international cooperation, Europeans as a whole are roughly divided as to whether their global interests are in line with those of the US – while those in Germany, France and the UK are much more sceptical. European opinion is overwhelming that China's interests are not consistent with their own when it comes to dealing with the effects of globalisation.

As in the US, globalisation and international economic cooperation are not particularly popular in Europe. While views vary from country to country, and issue area to issue area, public opinion in Europe is wary enough about involvement in the world economy – let alone substantial increases in openness or in international cooperation – to make it difficult for European policymakers to undertake substantial initiatives without being able to demonstrate a measurable, direct pay-off to their constituents.

Table 5.4 Attitudes towards trade in the US, France and China

Question: Overall, do you think international trade is good or bad for... (percentage responding in each category, 'don't know' omitted)

	US	France	China
The economy			
good (%)	57	65	92
bad (%)	43	35	8
Companies			
good (%)	54	56	86
bad (%)	46	44	14
Consumers like you			
good (%)	73	62	80
bad (%)	27	38	20
Creating jobs			
good (%)	38	26	81
bad (%)	62	74	19
The environment			
good (%)	48	31	66
bad (%)	52	69	34
Job security for workers			
good (%)	31	19	75
bad (%)	69	81	25

Source: The Chicago Council on Global Affairs/WorldPublicOpinion.org, Apr 2007. Available at *http:// www.thechicagocouncil.org/UserFiles/File/POS_Topline%20Reports/POS%202007_Globalization%20and%20 Trade/2007%20GlobTrade_quaire.pdf* (accessed 26 Mar 2012).

Table 5.5 Public opinion in the European Union (percentage responding in each category)

Question	EU		Germany		France		UK	
	Agree	Disagree	Agree	Disagree	Agree	Disagree	Agree	Disagree
Globalisation is an opportunity for economic growth	67	33	70	30	52	48	78	22
Globalisation increases social inequalities	72	28	76	24	84	16	66	34
The EU and the USA have the same interests when dealing with globalisation	52	48	44	56	40	60	43	57
Globalisation is profitable for large companies, not for citizens	73	27	68	32	85	15	74	26
The EU and China have the same interests when dealing with globalisation	31	69	24	76	17	83	26	74

Source: Standard Eurobarometer Report 73, 'Public Opinion in the European Union', Nov 2010. Available at *http://ec.europa.eu/public_opinion/archives/eb/eb73/eb73_anx_full.pdf* (accessed 26 Mar 2012).

5.3   China

The 'Chinese development model' is a variant of the 'Asian development model', probably first articulated by Japan in the 1960s, and shares features with such other periods of rapid growth as Germany during the 1930s, Brazil during the 1960s and 1970s, and the USSR in the 1950s and 1960s. These policies can generate tremendous early growth, but they also can lead to deep imbalances.

At the heart of the models are large subsidies for manufacturing, meant to increase investment in manufacturing capacity, generate employment growth and provide high profits to private or public investors. In nearly every case these subsidies are paid for by the household sector. China used three mechanisms to this end, following the model pioneered by Japan in its postwar boom.

The first mechanism is to constrain wage growth to well below the growth in labour productivity. During the past decade, wages have slightly more than doubled, while productivity nearly tripled. The gap is maintained with the help of the huge pool of surplus labour in the countryside; prohibitions on meaningful labour organisation; and the creation of an underclass of migrant workers who lack legal residence permits (*hukou*) and therefore have virtually no legal protections. Lagging wage growth represented a transfer from workers to employers, effectively subsidising businesses, increasing production, constraining household income and consumption, and thus forcing up the domestic savings rate.

The second mechanism is an undervalued exchange rate, which has prevailed since the massive devaluation of the renminbi in 1994, especially given soaring productivity. The undervaluation of the RMB functions as a substantial consumption tax imposed on all imported goods, and on consumers more generally. The principal beneficiaries are manufacturers in the tradable goods sector, heavily concentrated in Guangdong and the coastal provinces.

The third mechanism to boost manufacturing is severe financial repression. Almost all household savings in China are in the form of bank deposits, and the monetary authorities control banks, determining the direction of credit, risks and interest rates. The People's Bank of China, following instructions of the State Council, sets the maximum deposit rate and the minimum lending rate. These rates effectively transfer resources from depositors to borrowers. For example, in the past decade nominal lending rates have averaged little more than 6% even as the economy grew nominally by 14–16% annually. Household deposits (including farm deposits) have been anywhere from 80% to 100% of GDP. The minimum spread between the deposit rate and the lending rate is also set very high in order to guarantee the banks a large and safe profit; excessive spreads are estimated to be roughly equal to 1% of GDP. Overall, the combined interest-rate related transfers of 4–9% of GDP represent a very high hidden tax on households.

All three of these mechanisms do the same thing, albeit by distributing the costs and benefits in different ways to different groups among households and producers. They effectively tax household income and use the proceeds to subsidise producers, infrastructure investors, real estate developers, local and provincial borrowers, central government borrowers – in fact anyone who has access to bank lending, who employs workers, or who manufactures tradable goods, whether or not they actually export them.

The policies were of course successful at generating very rapid GDP growth, driven by high levels of investment. They also resulted in large trade surpluses as a consequence of consumption-constraining polices that pushed up the savings rate. Domestically, the impact of these policies was reflected in the extraordinarily low and declining share of GDP represented by household consumption. In the 1980s household consumption represented about 50–52% of GDP, which was far below that of developed countries and Latin America, but in line with that of other Asian export-driven economies. As indicated in Figure 5.1, over the course of the 1990s, Chinese consumption declined further, to reach a meagre 46% of GDP by 2000. And by 2005 household consumption in China had dropped to an astonishing 40% of GDP.

Figure 5.1 China's household consumption and government expenditure as share of GDP

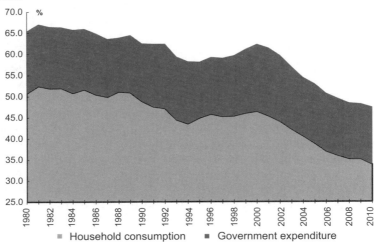

Source: China Statistical Yearbook 2011.

This eventually prompted policymakers to pledge during 2005 that they would take every step necessary to raise household consumption to help rebalance the economy. They expressed concern that such low levels of domestic consumption implied excessive reliance on the trade surplus to generate growth. But there was no political consensus in favour of taking the steps necessary to change course, and Beijing found it next to impossible to increase consumption without abandoning the investment and export-driven growth model altogether. Despite the expressed desire to reverse the trend, by 2010, the last year for which we have complete statistics, household consumption had fallen further to just 34% of GDP.

The counterpart to the very low level of consumption has been the high and rising level of savings. Household savings are high in part due to the underdeveloped financial system and lack of an effective social insurance safety net. After bouncing around between 10% and 20% of disposable income in the 1980s, around 1992 household savings began rising steadily until 1998, stabilising at around 24-26%. But the real increase in national savings in recent years has been due to a sharp rise in corporate and government savings. Of course, investment rose steadily during this period from around 23% of GDP in 1990 until it reached 50% in 2011.

All this led to the well-known dramatic evolution of China's trade position, from small surpluses or deficits until 1996, followed by a steady upward march of its trade surplus. This reached around 5% of China's GDP in 2003, after which it surged to over 10% of GDP in 2007–8. The Great Recession led to a collapse in global demand, which brought the surplus down, but the underlying conditions that create enormous Chinese surpluses have not changed drastically.

The result of this model is so much investment-driven and employment-generating growth that even with massive transfers from households, household income has grown dramatically. For the past decade, while the country was clocking growth rates of 10–12% annually, household income grew 7–9% annually. So why not continue this growth model forever?

The model cannot be sustained, for at least three reasons, two internal and one external. The obvious internal constraint is that rapid economic development has put major upward pressure on labour costs, which undermines export growth. The other internal constraint is on investment, which begins to bind as development progresses. When the capital stock is small and of very low quality, as was the case in China in 1979, almost any increase in capital stock is likely to increase labour productivity. But over time, it becomes more and more likely that cheap capital and socialised credit fund economically wasteful projects. The investments are profitable for those who make them, while the costs are spread through the entire country. China cannot simply continue to subsidise investment at the levels of the past and expect it to be of a type and quality justified by the country's needs.

The third constraint is in the foreign sector. Sustaining the current policy mix will continue to require large trade surpluses. As long as the rest of the world – primarily the US and the deficit countries of Europe and Latin America – were able to absorb China's exports, the fact that domestic households bought a declining share of Chinese production did not much matter. But by 2007 China's trade surplus as a share of global GDP had become the highest recorded in 100 years, perhaps ever, and the rest of the world found it increasing difficult to absorb it. To make matters worse, the global financial crisis sharply reduced the ability and willingness of other countries to maintain current trade deficits, and this downward pressure on China's current account surplus is likely to continue.

So China has hit all three constraints – labour costs have risen, capital is wasted, and the world is finding it increasingly difficult to absorb Chinese exports. For all its past success, China now needs to revise its development model, and the sooner it does so the less painful the adjustment will be. China needs to raise wages, interest rates and the value of the currency in order to reverse the flow of wealth from the household sector to the state and corporate sector. This will run into opposition from the beneficiaries of this flow; and it could also cause financial distress to those businesses that have become heavily dependent on the previous strategy. In the context of an already weak banking system, this raises the spectre of problems in the country's financial system.

The historical precedents for this kind of adjustment are not encouraging. There is reason for concern that China will adjust too slowly, and that the troubled and contentious adjustment will lead to lower growth rates. A small but rising number of Chinese economists are now beginning to predict sharply lower annual growth rates of 6–7% over the next few years.

All this suggests some concern for the future of China's economic growth. For the country to change course requires a rate of increase of consumption that seems unlikely without a major transformation of China's economic and political circumstances. This is of course possible, but given political constraints it may be unrealistic to expect it. The Chinese growth model has been a great success in many ways. It has created an economic structure with major stakes in a continuation, and a whole range of actors with strong interests in keeping it going. While pressures for change abroad and at home promise to grow, it is not clear that the Chinese political and economic order are in a position to respond effectively to these pressures.

We can perhaps see this most clearly in the issue of financial sector reform. For the past decade there has been a spirited discussion on the need to reform the financial services industry, culminating in widely noted and controversial comments by Premier Wen Jiabao on the need to break up the monopoly of the big banks, force a more competitive cost structure and divert lending from the state sector to the private sector. This call for reform was not driven by the global financial crisis. For Beijing, the need to reform the country's financial system is driven almost wholly by internal considerations – most specifically the growing perception that credit growth has largely benefited the least efficient parts of the economy at the expense of the very efficient small and medium enterprises.

The debate over financial reform, and the fact that it is being driven largely by internal considerations and not by the need for external coordination, suggests more generally that China's perception of the need for global coordination is likely to be trumped by domestic concerns. In the view of Beijing, the key international failing that led to the global crisis was due not to the existence of trade imbalances driven by excess savings, but rather to the role of the US dollar as the global reserve currency. In Beijing's view, the dominance of the US dollar allowed and even encouraged the US to initiate the imbalances, driven largely in the form of a consumption boom. Beijing has urged Washington to address its low domestic savings and large fiscal deficit as a precondition to global stability, although it has not been made clear how this would be consistent with China's continued reliance on exports to the US.

In spite of significant divergences from other major economies in its understanding of the causes of the crisis, however, there is nonetheless some basis for hoping for Chinese cooperation in global initiatives. Since Premier Wen Jiabao famously called China's economy 'unsteady, unbalanced, uncoordinated and unsustainable' in early 2007, Beijing has accepted publically that it must wean the Chinese economy from its excessive reliance on investment to generate growth, and replace it with domestic consumption. Reducing the growth rate of investment is relatively easy, but causing consumption growth to surge has proved extremely difficult. Given the disproportionate importance of investment and trade in generating domestic demand, it will be very difficult for China to reduce investment growth at the same time as the external account is weakening without suffering a major decline in growth.

5.4 Brazil

We take Brazil as roughly symbolic of many democratic developing countries that have generally embraced integration into the international economy. Latin America's biggest economy has been doing reasonably well lately, despite some trying times in the 1990s. Economic reform has continued, both under the centre-left government of Fernando Henrique Cardoso, and the somewhat more leftist governments of the succeeding Workers' Party presidents, Luiz Inácio ('Lula') da Silva and Dilma Rousseff. The economy has benefited from a substantial commodity boom, with dramatic improvements in the terms of trade and large export surpluses. Economic growth has been coupled with a continuation of social reforms that have aimed at reducing the country's very unequal income distribution.

Brazil is something of a paragon of an economically open, progressive political economy that has been able both to participate in world markets and to engage in some important social reforms. In this, it can be contrasted with governments, including some in neighbouring countries, that have turned away from 'globalisation' and taken a militantly populist, often anti-globalisation, stance. Notable among these in the past decade have been Venezuela, Ecuador, Bolivia and Argentina; and there are many non-Latin American examples. In comparison to these turns towards traditional populist nationalism, Brazil represents a combination of sympathy for globalisation, commitment to greater social equity, and stable democratic politics.

Nonetheless, at least some of Brazil's achievements have been due to favourable external conditions. Rapid growth in East Asia has fuelled demand for Brazilian raw materials and agricultural products, and has been a major contributor to the country's growth even during the troubled years after 2007. Between a major increase in the country's export volumes and a substantial improvement in its terms of trade, Brazil's exports in 2010 were nearly triple what they had been 2002. Perhaps more important, the country's trade has been strongly reoriented towards East Asia: in 2000, Brazilian exports to the US were more than ten times what they were to China, while by 2010 the nation's exports to China were more than twice what they were to the US.

This means that a major portion of economic growth in Brazil – and in other major commodity-exporting nations – relies on a continuation of rapid manufacturing growth in Asia, which in turn may depend upon rapid export growth. Inasmuch as one doubts the long-term prospects for sustaining the rate of export and manufacturing expansion in Asia, this calls into question the continuation of patterns and rates of economic growth in Brazil.

Another dimension is that of the country's enduring social problems. Poverty and criminality remain serious problems in the country's major cities, and are the focus of much political attention.

Brazil has never been particularly passionate about its involvement in the global economy. The country is large and rich in resources, and has a very large and developed business community and middle class – neither of which has traditionally seen itself as heavily engaged with the rest of the world economy.

While Brazil has not in recent decades gone down the populist path of, say, Argentina or Venezuela, there are social and political forces that could conceivably push it more in that direction. Even if it stays on its current course, the country is hardly a globalisation enthusiast; it is more of a reticent fellow traveller.

Over the coming decades, the Brazilian government will need to deal with the likelihood that commodity exports will not sustain the country's economic growth, and with the nation's continuing social divisions. Brazil continues to aspire for leadership in Latin America, and in the world more generally. Nonetheless, the country's concerns differ substantially from those of the developed world. Despite its advances, Brazil is very much a developing country, whose interests are first and foremost in securing opportunities for its further growth. It is very unlikely to be willing, or able, to play a leadership role in managing international economic affairs.

We return to the role of large developing nations such as Brazil and China in the international system, their preferences, and their interests in global cooperation in Section 7.6.

5.5   Inconvenient truths

These brief surveys of the domestic political economy of the major centres of economic activity illustrate two simple, if inconvenient, truths. First, for the foreseeable future, most of the world's nations (and the European Union) will be primarily engaged in dealing with difficult internal economic, social and political problems. Second, for a variety of reasons, enthusiasm for international economic integration has waned substantially in almost every major region. On both accounts, then, it will be a struggle to sustain and increase the level of international economic collaboration. National policy will focus on national (or, in the case of the EU, on European) problems. And national publics appear poorly disposed to make serious compromises and sacrifices to shore up an international economic order about which they have grave doubts.

National policymakers in the advanced industrial countries face domestic audiences that are ambivalent about international economic integration, and that are wary even of their traditional economic partners. There are also powerful entrenched interests in many regions whose concerns may impede progress in international economic cooperation. Governments in the G7 also face large emerging economies whose views of the world, and whose domestic political constituencies, are often at odds with those of the industrialised world. Both realities are illustrated in Tables 5.6, 5.7 and 5.8 . Table 5.6 shows that while overwhelming majorities of the public in Brazil and China view international trade as favourable to their countries, bare majorities are pro-trade in Europe, while US opinion is even less favourable. Brazilians and Chinese, similarly, believe that their countries are well-positioned in international economic competition (Table 5.7), while such confidence is only shared unambiguously by the Germans; the British are divided, and the French and Americans decidedly pessimistic. Perhaps even more striking, and more directly relevant, Table 5.8 demonstrates that large majorities in the US, the UK and France regard the rise of such emerging economies as China and India as a threat rather than an opportunity (the Germans are split on the matter). All this highlights the fact that many national governments have a hard time convincing their people that it is worthwhile to forgo some national prerogatives in favour of global governance.

Most governments have had difficulties convincing their constituents to make significant sacrifices on behalf of international cooperation, and are likely to continue to face such difficulties. This makes it particularly important to identify the areas in which, and ways in which, initiatives for greater global governance are especially important. In light of the great political costs of obtaining national agreement on a further delegation of government functions to the global level, a clear sense is needed of where to focus the international community's efforts.

Table 5.6 Attitudes towards trade across countries

Is the development of international trade...

	US	UK	Germany	France	China	Brazil
Mainly a good thing for your country	39	62	50	53	90	76
Mainly a bad thing for your country	26	9	27	16	6	10
Neither one nor the other	35	29	23	31	4	14

Source: IFOP for La Croix, 'Perceptions towards Globalisation across Ten Countries', Jan 2011, available at *http://www.ifop.com/media/poll/1390-2-study_file.pdf* (accessed 12 Apr 2012).

Table 5.7 Views on national competitive position

How well positioned is your country in international economic competition?

	US	UK	Germany	France	China	Brazil
Well positioned	44	52	81	35	71	77
Poorly positioned	56	48	19	65	29	23

Note: Those who answered 'don't know' or 'no opinion' are excluded.
Source: As Table 5.6.

Table 5.8 Views towards emerging economies

Do you believe that the growth of countries like China and India is...

	US	UK	Germany	France
A serious threat to your country's companies and jobs	64	57	49	67
A great source of opportunities for your country to conquer new markets	36	43	51	33

Note: Those who answered 'don't know' or 'no opinion' are excluded.
Source: As Table 5.6.

6 The Normative Case for Governance of the International Economy

Global problems push us to think in terms of global solutions.[17] Discussions in the G20, WTO and other multilateral fora often proceed as if the correct remedy for our economic problems is always more global cooperation – more rules, more harmonisation, more discipline on national policies. But, as we have seen, there are major obstacles to the construction of robust global institutions. National sovereignty is zealously guarded, not least by domestic politicians who do not want to see their prerogatives eroded. And the challenge is not going to get easier in the years ahead. The rising powers of the world economy – China, India, Brazil and other emerging market economies – place if anything greater importance on national sovereignty than the traditional great powers. The practical and substantive challenges that global governance faces call for a more calibrated approach that focuses on areas where the need for building global institutions is greatest, while not wasting political or organisational capital in areas where the returns are small.

In this chapter, we present a taxonomy of economic policies to clarify what *is* and *is not* important to look for in international economic cooperation. The objective is to differentiate domains in which policy coordination is desirable (and more likely to be achievable) from issues where it is neither necessary nor achievable. We make a distinction in particular between two types of policies with global spillovers: 'beggar-thy-neighbour' policies, which aim to extract economic advantage at the expense of other nations, and 'beggar-thyself' policies where the economic costs, if any, are borne primarily at home. The latter call for global oversight that is weaker and qualitatively different.

6.1 New modes of global governance?

We begin with a quick review of the state of thinking on global governance. There was extensive discussion of effective models of global governance even before the international financial crisis struck, with policymakers as well as academics proffering visions of new forms of governance that leave the nation-state behind. Few of these models envisage a truly global version of the nation-state; a global

---

17   This section draws on Rodrik (2011b, ch 10) and Rodrik (2012).

legislature or council of ministers is too much of a fantasy. The solutions on offer rely instead on new conceptions of political community, representation and accountability. The hope is that these innovations can replicate many of constitutional democracy's essential functions at the global level.

The crudest forms of such global governance envisage straightforward transfers of national powers to international technocrats. Economists appear to be particularly enamoured of such arrangements. For example, when the European economics network VoxEU.org solicited advice from leading economists on how to address the frailties of the global financial system in the wake of the 2008 crisis, the proposed solutions often took the form of tighter international rules administered by some kind of technocracy: an international bankruptcy court, a world financial organisation, an international bank charter, an international lender of last resort, and so on (see Eichengreen and Baldwin, 2008).

Others, such as international lawyer and political scientist Anne-Marie Slaughter, have focused on transnational networks created by regulators, judges, and even legislators. These networks can perform governance functions even when they are not constituted as intergovernmental organisations or formally institutionalised. Such networks, Slaughter argues, extend the reach of formal governance mechanisms, allow persuasion and information sharing across national borders, contribute to the formation of global norms, and can generate the capacity to implement international norms and agreements in nations where the domestic capacity to do so is weak (Slaughter 2004). The club of central bankers centred at the Bank for International Settlements is a premier example of such a network.

John Ruggie has emphasised the parallel role that global civil society can play, enunciating norms of corporate social responsibility in human rights, labour practices, health, anti-corruption and the environment. The United Nations' Global Compact, which Ruggie had a big hand in shaping, embodies this agenda. The Compact aims to transform international corporations into vehicles for social and economic progress. The goal is to allow the private sector to shoulder some of the functions that states are finding increasingly difficult to finance and carry out, as in public health and environmental protection, narrowing the governance gap between international markets and national governments (Ruggie, 2004).

Joshua Cohen and Charles Sabel have gone even further in outlining a future in which accountability takes a truly global form. They envisage global deliberative processes among regulators which feed into the development of a global political community, with people coming to share a common identity as members of an 'organized global populace' (Cohen and Sabel, 2005, p. 796). At the end of the day, true global governance requires individuals who feel that they are global citizens.

The nation-state does not have many defenders. As Sen puts it, 'there is something of a tyranny of ideas in seeing the political divisions of states (primarily, national states) as being, in some way, fundamental, and in seeing them not only as practical constraints to be addressed, but as divisions of basic significance in ethics and political philosophy' (Sen, 2009, p 143). At the same time, political authority still remains vested for the most part in national governments.

The global governance arrangements described above require the transfer of substantial authority from national institutions to transnational, multinational or multilateral entities. Arguments on behalf of new forms of global governance – whether of the direct subordination, network, or corporate social responsibility type – raise difficult questions. To whom are these mechanisms accountable? From where do these global clubs of regulators, international non-governmental organisations or large firms get their mandates? Who empowers and polices them? What ensures that the voice and interests of those who are less globally networked are also heard? In a nation-state, the electorate is the ultimate source of political mandates, and elections the ultimate vehicle for accountability. If you do not respond to your constituencies' expectations and aspirations, you are voted out. The democratic state is tried and tested. Its global counterpart sounds too experimental and utopian.[18]

6.2   Thinking about global governance: first principles

Going back to basics, the principle of 'subsidiarity' provides the right way of thinking about issues of global governance. It tells us which kinds of policies should be coordinated or harmonised globally and which should be left largely to domestic decision-making. The principle demarcates areas where we need extensive global governance and areas where only a thin layer of global rules is adequate. We can think of this as a choice between a WTO-type (thick) global regime versus a GATT-type (thin) regime.

The premise in what follows is that any practical mechanism of global governance must rely on the willingness of national governments to submit to international discipline. Nation-states, the primary decision-making units in the world economy, must be provided with a reason why it is in their interest to cooperate and coordinate, rather than go it alone. Transnational altruism is not a reliable pillar on which to construct global governance.

6.3   A quartet of policy problems

To see how the principle of subsidiarity applies, we make a distinction between four different variants of economic policies. We start from the two extremes, 'purely domestic policies' and 'global commons policies', which are the easiest to describe and have the most direct implications for global governance. Then we turn to the trickier intermediate cases, which we call 'beggar-thy-neighbour' and 'beggar-thyself' policies.

---

18 For example, it is interesting that Slaughter's (2004) most telling illustrations of networked global governance come from the area of financial markets. She points to the International Organization of Securities Commissions (IOSCO) and the Basel Committee on Banking Supervision as networks of regulators that set global rules for financial markets. Most economists would say, however, that these institutions have failed to deliver an adequate set of rules. Many would also argue that they have been too dominated by financial industry interests and that the Basel Committee's capital adequacy rules have in fact played a contributing role in both the Asian financial crisis of 1997/8 and the global financial crisis of 2008/9.

6.4 Purely domestic policies

At one extreme are domestic policies that create no (or very few) direct spillovers across national borders. Examples are educational policies, highway safety standards and urban zoning. Since the object of regulation in both instances is a non-traded service (human capital, local transport and real estate, respectively), such policies do not affect the economic interests of other countries, at least directly. They therefore require no international agreement and can be safely left to domestic policymakers. This seems to be widely accepted, as there is little clamour for internationalisation of regulation in such areas.

Of course, in practice regulations in non-traded markets influence the rest of the economy and therefore have implications for other nations as well. Highway safety standards, for example, can affect the demand for oil and its price on world markets.[19] Nothing is purely domestic when general equilibrium implications are taken into account. But it is understood or presumed that such effects are indirect and uncertain, and that the policies have no intent to discriminate against foreign economic interests.

6.5 Global commons policies

At the other end are policies that relate to 'global commons', such as global climate. The characteristic of a global commons is that the outcome for each nation is determined not by domestic policies, but by (the sum total of) other countries' policies. The classic case is greenhouse gas emissions. Global climate is a pure global public good, in that no country can be excluded from benefiting from the control of greenhouse gases in other countries, and nor can a country keep the benefits of such policies to itself.

There is a very strong case for establishing global rules in these policy domains, since it is in the interest of each country, left to its own devices, to neglect its share of the upkeep of the global commons. Absent a binding agreement, the rational strategy for any small country is to free ride on other countries' emissions policies. Since each country reasons the same way, the decentralised outcome is one where no country invests in costly climate control policies. Hence failure to reach global agreement would condemn all to a collective disaster.[20] That is why there is no alternative to global governance in the area of climate change, difficult as it may be to achieve.

True global public goods are rare. Even though the global economy is often portrayed in a similar light, in fact few economic policies qualify as 'global commons policies' in the sense sketched out above. We commonly hear statements to the effect that 'a growing, open world economy is a global public good'. The idea seems to be that as each nation pursues its own narrow interests,

---

19 And one of the most significant disputes between NAFTA partners was the US–Mexico conflict over Mexican truckers' access to US highways.

20 Large countries have some incentive to control emissions, to the extent that their contribution to the global stock of greenhouse is non-trivial.

the world economy would slide into rampant protectionism and everyone would lose as a result.

But this logic relies on a false analogy of the global economy as a global commons. What makes global warming a global rather than national problem, requiring global cooperation, is that the globe has a single climate system. It makes no difference where the carbon is emitted. One might say that all our economies are similarly intertwined, and no doubt that would be true to an important extent. But in the case of global warming, domestic restrictions on carbon emissions provide no or little benefit at home. By contrast, good economic policies – including openness – benefit the home economy first and foremost. The economic fortunes of individual nations are determined largely by what happens at home rather than abroad. If open economy policies are desirable it's because openness is in a nation's own self-interest – not because it helps others. Openness and other good policies that contribute to global economic stability rely on self-interest, not on global spirit.

Free trade and appropriate financial regulations at the national level are desirable, regardless of the policies of other countries. If other countries also follow 'good' policies, all the better for us. But unlike with climate change, there is no logic that suggests countries will systematically follow policies that are harmful to the world economy. In fact, quite the contrary.

However, there are two caveats. First, sometimes domestic economic advantage comes at the expense of other nations. Second, there is no guarantee that countries will do what is economically right for themselves, for reasons of domestic politics gone awry or sheer ignorance. These exceptions give us two intermediate cases between purely domestic policies and global commons, which we analyse under the headings of 'beggar-thy-neighbour policies' and 'beggar-thyself policies'.

6.6 Beggar-thy-neighbour policies

A nation with 'beggar-thy-neighbour' policies derives an economic benefit at the expense of other nations. The purest illustration occurs when a dominant supplier of a natural resource, such as oil, restricts supply on world markets so as to drive up world prices. In this instance the exporter's gain is the rest of the world's loss, and there is an additional global deadweight loss due to the supply restriction. A similar mechanism operates with the so-called 'optimum tariff', with which a large country manipulates its terms of trade by placing tariffs on its imports. There is a clear case in these instances for global coordination taking the form of limiting or prohibiting the use of such policies.

In some instances, beggar-thy-neighbour effects may be intermingled with other, domestic motives. Consider for example currency undervaluation, which is often treated as a mercantilist policy aimed at extracting economic advantage from other countries. China's motive in pursuing such a policy seems to have been primarily to accelerate its economic growth by promoting structural change from low- to high-productivity areas. To the extent that this policy generates an external surplus, it requires that other nations are willing to bear the counterpart deficits. But in what sense does this impart a harm to other countries? In the case of China's currency policies, for example, it was often asserted prior to the global financial crisis that there was a willing partner in the US. The US trade deficit allowed it to borrow and finance its consumption and credit boom on the cheap, while China subsidised its exports through a cheap renminbi. There were some complaints in the US from those adversely affected by China's exports. But these complaints were drowned by those who argued that the relationship was mutually beneficial, even if of doubtful sustainability.

Global imbalances have become a much more serious issue in the aftermath of the financial crisis, as we discuss elsewhere in the report. It now seems clear that large current account surpluses such as those of China have contributed to financial fragility. There is also concern due to the spike in unemployment in the US and Europe. When the economy looks as if it is caught in a Keynesian situation of excess supply, external deficits contribute to the deficiency of aggregate demand and aggravate unemployment. Paul Krugman famously wrote in 2009 that 'we're looking at 1.4 million US jobs lost due to Chinese mercantilism' (Krugman, 2009). Whether there is such a direct link or not, currency policies that export unemployment and financial instability increasingly look like beggar-thy-neighbour policies. They are an area where global cooperation and coordination becomes necessary, at least among systemically large countries.

Rules with regard to bank secrecy or the taxation of capital present other instances where there is a mix of considerations. A jurisdiction that is set up as a pure tax haven, with the sole objective of attracting deposits and capital from abroad, can be said to gain economic advantage at the expense of other nations and to follow beggar-thy-neighbour policies. But what if a nation views low taxes or strict secrecy as 'correct' policies to follow *for domestic reasons*, regardless of consequences for cross-border flows of money? Then, even if such policies have adverse effects on others, the case for global coordination is significantly weakened (as we discuss below under 'beggar- thyself policies'). Disciplining low-tax jurisdictions under such considerations would require, at a minimum, an account of how a *global* economic loss is created in the absence of coordination.

Analytically, it helps to distinguish between the level of a policy that is domestically optimal absent cross-border interactions, and the increment in that policy that becomes desirable once those interactions are taken into account. There should be a much higher threshold for disciplining the first component. Take tariffs, for example. Suppose t is the domestically second-best level of taxation in an economy (due to, say, revenue reasons), holding the external terms of trade constant. Assume that the optimal level of the tariff becomes $t' = t + dt$ once external terms-of-trade effects are taken into account. The dt component of the tariff is the pure beggar-thy-neighbour component, which ought to be regulated internationally. There is much less ground for international discipline on t, unless other countries can demonstrate significant negative spillovers which more than offset the benefits to the home country.

6.7 Beggar-thyself policies

Beggar-thy-neighbour policies have to be distinguished from what we may call 'beggar-thyself' policies. The latter are policies whose economic costs are borne primarily at home, even though they may produce effects also on others. Examples are agricultural subsidies, bans on genetically-modified organisms, or lax financial regulation. In each instance, there may be costs to other countries. But these policies are deployed not to extract advantages from other nations, but because other competing policy objectives at home – such as distributional, administrative, public health or other political concerns – dominate the economic motives.

Consider, for example, agricultural subsidies in Europe. Economists generally agree that these are inefficient and that the benefits to European farmers come at large costs to everyone else. Economists also agree that the bulk of those costs are paid by European residents, in the form of high prices, high taxes, or both. The subsidies do produce spillovers to other nations. Agricultural producers around the world get hurt, while consumers of agriculture benefit.

Even though the presence of such spillovers is often taken to establish a case for global governance over these policies – as in the Doha Round of trade negotiations – it is not clear why that should be so. There can be two reasons for the pursuit of beggar-thyself policies: there can be compensating non-economic benefits, or the government in question can be simply making a mistake. Let us consider each of these two possibilities in turn.

Say that European governments have decided the economic costs of agricultural subsidies are worth paying for as the price for sustaining healthy rural farming communities. Even though the policy is economically inefficient, in this case it serves a broader social purpose and therefore is 'optimal', from Europe's own perspective. A direct implication is that any global effort to reduce or eliminate these subsidies would leave Europe worse off. Even if such an attempt were to produce net economic benefits to the rest of the world, it would come at the expense of socio-economic losses for Europe. Thus there would seem to be a very weak case for global discipline.

The same logic applies to bans on genetically modified organisms or hormone-fed beef, where the perceived compensating benefit at home is precaution against health risks. It also applies broadly to the conduct of industrial policies by developing nations, where the intent is to reap the dynamic benefits of more rapid structural change and economic diversification. In none of these cases does it seem appropriate to empower the 'global community' to tell individual nations how they ought to weight competing goals.

This doesn't preclude a global conversation over the nature of diverse benefits and harms to the parties. Such conversations can be helpful in reducing international misunderstanding about the objective of policies, and sometime in establishing new behavioural norms. But global restraints on domestic policy space would seem inappropriate since there is no prima facie reason why the economic interests of other nations ought to take precedence over the social-economic benefits to the home nation. Once again, it is unclear whether the net benefit to the world from global discipline is positive.

The case against global regulation becomes even stronger when the spillovers to the rest of the world are, on balance, positive. This may seem unlikely, but note that it is indeed the case with export subsidies in agriculture. Economic analysis suggests that such subsidies improve the terms of trade of the rest of the world and are therefore a 'gift' from a country to its trade partners. Some countries or groups are harmed, of course. But it is difficult to see why this should be a reason for restraining home country policies. Consider an analogous situation where a country decides, unilaterally, to reduce its import tariffs. Similar to the export subsidy case, some other nations – those who import similar things – may well get hurt. Yet economists, reasonably, would never contemplate enacting global rules that restrict a country's ability to liberalise its trade!

Let's now go to the second case where the country in question has actually made a 'mistake'. Suppose agricultural subsidies are an unambiguously bad idea, even when all the other potential non-economic benefits are taken into account. Yet somehow the country's political system fails, and delivers a bad policy. Indeed, there is no guarantee that domestic policies accurately reflect societal demands. Policymakers may be short-sighted, ignorant or captured. Even democracies are frequently taken hostage by special interests.

One class of policy failures is easy to deal with, at least conceptually. These are failures due to time inconsistency, in which the policymakers' incentive to give in to short-term temptation results in long-term losses. Trying to generate 'surprise' inflation or protectionist horse-trading among legislators are well-known examples. Many nations deal with time-inconsistency failures through 'delegation', the transfer of authority to an autonomous body – an independent central bank or tariff-setting authority – that is less susceptible to the push and pull of daily politics. International disciplines can play the same insulating role too.

At the same time, in democracies delegation takes place only under a narrow range of circumstances. We tend to see delegation domestically when there is little distributive conflict over the objectives of policy, the issues are technical rather than political, and the 'chain of delegation' can be kept short. Delegating rule-making to an autonomous body so everyone can be better off is one thing; delegating so one political party gains at the expense of another is something else altogether. Moreover, it is not clear why international delegation should hold an advantage over the domestic kind, even when those conditions are satisfied. Policy discipline exerted by an extranational body may or may not be more effective than discipline exerted domestically. The case for global governance on account of time inconsistency is at best a qualified one.

Things get even more complicated when policy failures do not derive from a simple time inconsistency. To be sure, both domestic and foreign welfare would be enhanced if global rules could be designed that prevent mistaken policies from being adopted. One problem is that similar or worse policy failures can take place at the international level as well. For example, most economists would agree that banking interests and pharmaceutical companies have exerted too much influence in setting Basel capital adequacy rules and WTO intellectual property rules, respectively.

Another problem is that it is not easy in practice to distinguish domestic policy failures from non-economic considerations. Technocratic governance at the global level may fail to reflect adequately the kind of non-efficiency objectives that play a role in democracies, as in the agricultural subsidy context for example. In other words, technocrats (trade lawyers, economists, financial specialists) may substitute their own normative judgements for those of democratic polities.

These issues come into full play in the area of financial regulation. It is widely accepted that regulatory practices in a number of jurisdictions – the US, in particular – failed to rein in excessive leverage and risk-taking in the shadow banking system. The failure was of a beggar-thyself type, even though the consequences were amply felt throughout the rest of the world as well. The attempt to address the problem through internationally coordinated and harmonised financial regulations has borne some fruit, mainly in the form of Basel III. But as we have discussed, expectations about international cooperation were not fully realised and much of the real action in terms of new regulations took place nationally (or within a subset of EU members) in an uncoordinated manner.

The slow progress of global governance in this area reflects genuine differences in preferences over how finance should be regulated. The US, Britain, Switzerland and France/Germany have taken their own different paths because their financial systems differ and are the product of varying circumstances. Switzerland feels it can afford much higher capital requirements than others. France and Germany believe it is politically important to institute an international financial transaction tax. The US thinks restrictions on proprietary trading by banks would diminish financial fragility. Emerging markets have their own special concerns with hot money inflows. None of these positions is obviously right or wrong.

A central trade-off here is between financial innovation and financial stability. A light approach to regulation will maximise the scope for financial innovation (the development of new financial products), but at the cost of increasing the likelihood of financial crises and crashes. Strong regulation will reduce the incidence and costs of crises, but potentially at the cost of raising the cost of finance and excluding many from its benefits. There is no single optimal point along this trade-off. Requiring that communities whose preferences over the innovation–stability continuum vary all settle on the same solution might have the virtue that it reduces transaction costs in finance, but it would come at the cost of imposing arrangements that are out of sync with local preferences. The appropriate form of financial regulation depends on national circumstances and preferences, and cannot be determined in a uniform, technocratic manner.

The preference for domestic action also reflects in part the disappointing experience with previous international agreements. Basel I and Basel II both had flaws, that in some ways contributed to subsequent crises – by encouraging short-term debt (prior to the Asian financial crisis) and by endorsing reliance on banks' own risk models (prior to the global financial crisis). Many economists feel international banks have exerted too much influence in softening capital adequacy and other requirements in Basel III. It is by no means clear that the technocratic perspective that dominates the Basel process has served the global financial system well. Stronger democratic accountability to national parliaments may reduce banks' influence and base regulations on the preferences of a wider group of domestic constituencies.

Since in any case there is no analytical consensus on how to regulate financial markets, experimentation at the national level is of independent value. Even if national preferences were perfectly aligned, the world would benefit from the learning generated by a process of trial-and-error in different jurisdictions. As argued by Nicholas Dorn, professor at Erasmus School of Law, 'democratically-fuelled regulatory diversity is a safeguard against the recently experienced frenzy in global financial regulation and markets' (Dorn, 2009).

So fixing *domestic* policy failures by setting global rules on acceptable policy is problematic, both in theory and in practice. But we can envisage another type of global discipline which acts directly on the relevant margin. We have in mind procedural requirements designed to enhance the quality of domestic policymaking. Global disciplines pertaining to transparency, broad representation, accountability and use of scientific/economic evidence in domestic proceedings – without constraining the end result – are examples of such requirements.

Disciplines of this type are already in use in the WTO to some extent. The Agreements on Safeguards and Anti-Dumping specify domestic procedures that need to be followed when a government contemplates restricting imports from trade partners. Similarly the SPS Agreement on sanitary and phytosanitary measures explicitly requires the use of scientific evidence when health concerns are at issue. Procedural rules of this kind can be used much more extensively and to greater effect to enhance the quality of domestic decision-making. For example, anti-dumping rules can be improved by requiring that consumer and producer interests that would be adversely affected by the imposition of import duties take part in domestic proceedings. Subsidy rules can be improved by requiring economic cost-benefit analyses. Domestic financial regulation can be enhanced by global norms that emphasise transparent procedural rules limiting the influence of financial interests.

6.8   Summarising the typology

To summarise, different types of policies call for different responses at the global level. The conceptual framework laid out here suggests the following typology of optimal global regimes:

1. Purely domestic policies require no global action.
b. Global commons require globally harmonised policy regimes. (Example: a global set of rules that allocate emission permits.)
c. Beggar-thy-neighbour policies require the regulation of cross-border spillovers. (Examples: tariff bindings and restrictions on maximum size of current account deficits/surpluses.)

d. Beggar-thyself policies require global regimes aimed at enhancing the quality of domestic decision-making. (Examples: rules pertaining to transparency, representativeness, accountability and use of scientific/economic evidence in domestic proceedings.)

The previous chapter summarised some of the political-economy barriers that can make international economic cooperation – global governance – difficult. Domestic political constraints can stand in the way of even the most desirable global actions; and it is neither prudent nor practical simply to ignore these constraints. Rather, we should recognize how limited is the room for manoeuvre of major governments. In this chapter, we supplement our attempt at a realistic assessment of what is *possible* in the realm of global governance with a survey of what is *desirable* in this realm. Especially because meaningful collaboration is difficult, it is important to choose battles wisely. On the basis of our normative and positive analyses of prospects for international cooperation, we now turn to a survey of some of the issue areas we anticipate are likely to be at the centre of controversy over the coming period.

7 Macro is the New Trade: Future Problems of the International Economy

7.1 Introduction

The global economy could well suffer a major catastrophe over the next few years. A disorderly disintegration of the euro could trigger both a global recession and a tendency to reverse globalisation, setting back the commercial and financial integration that has been achieved over the last quarter of a century. Even if catastrophe is avoided, the international economy faces immense challenges. In this chapter we look at these challenges, of necessity briefly. We make the central point that even in the absence of catastrophe, tough choices will have to be made. We are particularly concerned about the opportunities, if any, that may arise to improve on what has become clearly dysfunctional and insufficient global governance.

It is now clear that the G20 cannot carry out its original reform agenda, whether in the short run or in the medium run. The question that remains is where to apply whatever political capital is available to pursue collective action. There is certainly no reason to pursue the issues that have been needlessly added to the agenda, particularly after the first Pittsburgh meeting. The question is which of the three main areas of concern contained in the original agenda require most direct attention. Should that limited political capital be applied to global financial governance? To the multilateral trading system? Or to macroeconomic policy coordination? In other words, where should the G20 apply its muscle to achieve the strong, sustainable and balanced growth that it has repeatedly purported to seek?

We argue that notwithstanding the desirability of strengthening the multilateral trading system and achieving global financial reform, whatever transformative capacity the G20 members have should be allocated first and foremost to improving macroeconomic policy coordination among themselves. We foresee the exacerbation of conflicts over national macroeconomic and, especially, currency policies, and also the persistence and recurrence of the global imbalances that characterised the decade leading up to the Great Recession. These problems must be attended through unprecedented collective action. Failure to do so would make it much harder – or even impossible – to address the trade and financial issues towards which the desired reforms in these areas are aimed. We argue that there is a strong normative case for enhanced economic policy cooperation, as well as a reasonable chance that it might be feasible. Finally, we supplement this point with a brief discussion of the role of developing countries in the world economy. We anticipate that they will face difficulties in the more constrained environment to come. To the extent that this raises issues of international conflict and cooperation, these largely fall under the rubric of macroeconomic policy coordination. We want ultimately to illustrate the tensions we expect, and the scope of desirable and feasible international cooperative action.

As we have indicated, progress on global economic cooperation confronts at least four major barriers. The first is the difficulty inherent in the provision of any global public good, as well as the other normative considerations that must be applied to the analysis of the suitability of supranational economic governance, as detailed in Chapter 6. The second set of obstacles, outlined in Chapter 5, is the complexity of the internal political and economic challenges faced by the world's major economic entities in the aftermath of the Great Recession, which present governments with great domestic challenges and little excess political capacity to take on new global commitments. The third impediment to greater cooperation is the great and increasing heterogeneity of goals among the major economic powers, especially as these powers have come to include emerging markets whose circumstances and preferences diverge in important ways from those of western Europe and North America. The final reason for caution in anticipating major new international initiatives is the disappointing record accumulated over the past decade, described in Chapter 4: optimistic anticipation has all too often given way to empty phrase-mongering.

All these considerations suggest the need for a healthy scepticism – an understanding of how difficult it will be for the major powers to devise further advances in global governance.

7.2 Trade

The crisis has, to the surprise of many, not led to a dramatic upsurge in protectionist policies. To be sure, governments have been confronted with political pressures to use trade policy to alleviate the impact of the crisis on their citizens.[21] Fortunately, until now those pressures have not led to a substantial increase in protectionism. Both Global Trade Alert (Evenett, 2011) and the OECD-WTO-UNCTAD 'Reports on G20 Trade and Investment Measures' report that practically every G20 country has undertaken protectionist actions despite repeated pledges, but those actions have not been quantitatively significant.

There are a number of explanations for the generally continued commitment to an open trading system. First, most major economies are now full members of the WTO and subject to its rules. As the WTO has some fairly serious

---

21   For one evaluation see Bown and Crowley (2012).

enforcement capabilities, this may have moderated governments' incentives to use trade protection as an early line of defence against the global financial crisis and ensuing recession. Second, trade protection is particularly (politically) well suited to sector-specific difficulties, such as the decline of a steel industry. The crisis had a broad impact on economic activity and employment, and while there were certainly industries that could have benefited from protection, most policymakers were more concerned about the broader macroeconomic blow that had been dealt to their countries. Finally, given what is at stake, it is conceivable that export sectors in the largest economies might have exercised their own political pressure to prevent protectionist actions by their governments that could have triggered retaliatory actions.

Nonetheless, the G20's failure to strengthen the multilateral trading system by concluding the Doha Round, as was solemnly promised, should be seen as a major cause of embarrassment and lack of credibility. If the prolonging of slow growth in the developed economies or any other circumstance were to unleash substantive protectionist actions, the G20 would come to regret deeply not having honoured its Doha commitments, even if those protectionist measures were kept within what is permitted by the WTO. The problem is that the excess of bound over applied tariffs, plus the latitude of other WTO disciplines in their present form, leave a huge space to sustain 'legal' protectionist interchanges that could have devastating economic effects. Providing insurance against this scenario all along has been the most significant – and least appreciated – value of a successful conclusion of the Doha Round.

Admittedly, however, the current political business cycle is not propitious for such an undertaking. Too many important electoral processes are underway, and unemployment rates in the developed countries are too high to allow for serious trade talks. It seems that for the foreseeable future it is unavoidable to continue relying only on the moratorium on additional trade and investment barriers agreed by the G20 (or, more cynically, the fear of retaliation within the WTO boundaries) that has so far allowed some reasonable preservation of open markets. Yet, unless there is a catastrophic shock to globalisation, we are confident that the time to conclude the Doha Round will come. What is already on the table, plus a modicum of political leadership and enlightenment to solve the still contentious issues, should allow for concluding the Doha Round, and this would finally leave the WTO in a position to deal with the other topics already posing a challenge to the multilateral trading system in this early part of the 21st century.

7.3 The challenge of financial regulatory coherence

The panic that hit the international financial system in 2008 was the first truly global financial crisis since the 1930s. The world was stunned by the speed with which what had appeared to be relatively minor, reasonably isolated problems in US housing finance led to the contemporary equivalent of a massive global bank run that threatened to shut down the entire enormous edifice of today's international financial markets. This extraordinary turn of events has, not surprisingly, provoked a widespread demand for reform of financial regulation, and the G20's early pledges of cooperation in designing and implementing such reforms, pledges that as we know have not been honoured.[22]

Surely, views differ as to the desirability of significantly greater coordination in reforming financial regulation systems. The system of regulation that is best for one country may not be well suited to another. Still, the unilateralist course taken by some of the reforms in the most significant jurisdictions may not be the best way to go if the global financial system is going to be sufficiently resilient. The complexity of the topics yet to be satisfactorily addressed is daunting. Dealing with liquidity standards, resolution regimes, OTC derivative markets and shadow banking, not to mention compliance with what has already been agreed, leaves a very open field for conflictual competition and even confrontation among different jurisdictions. The challenge is not about having exactly the same rules in every country. It is about providing enough coherence among the various national regulatory environments in a way that prevents regulatory arbitrage that could rapidly transform into a dangerous race to the bottom or – equally damaging – a 'spaghetti bowl' of contradictory, unsupervisable and unenforceable regulations.

And yet, without ceasing to monitor its evolution, financial reform does not seem to be a promising area in which the major powers might spend their marginal units of political capital. This observation is based on three considerations. One is that the institutions already in place, such as the FSB and the Basel Committee on Banking Supervision, along with the traditional collaborations among national regulators and central banks as well as the IMF, could conceivably be, if not optimal, at least enough to keep the reform effort broadly on track. Another is that if those mechanisms proved insufficient to provide for the necessary cooperation and the situation descended into a competition of incoherent reforms, the consequences for some financial jurisdictions would be so pernicious that some urgency for coordination would soon be restored. The third is that, at the present time, there appears to be very little political support for the harmonisation of financial regulations. Most major financial systems seem content to go their own ways, willing to confront issues of regulatory arbitrage by a combination of fine-tuning and managing flow so as to limit potentially pernicious race-to-the-bottom effects.

In fact, a reassertion of national control over finance is not necessarily a bad thing. It is better to have strong yet divergent domestic regulations than harmonised yet weak global regulations, even if we forfeit some of the benefits of financial integration as a result. The Eurozone has amply demonstrated the downsides of an intermediate outcome in which money and monetary policy become regional while fiscal and financial/regulatory regimes remain national. If Europe has failed to share sovereignty on such matters, it is unlikely that the rest of the world will do better anytime soon.

---

22   For one important study on the subject, see Goodhart *et al* (2012).

7.4   Conflicts over macroeconomic policy and related trade issues

This brings us to macroeconomic policies, and in particular to specific macroeconomic policies pursued by major economic powers that conflict with the goals of their partners. We expect a world in which job creation will be a crucial goal of every government, and all countries will attempt to promote exports and limit imports. In this context, we are likely to see increased tension over the macroeconomic policies of the major economies – in particular, over their exchange rate policies. And conflicts over exchange rates will feed into conflicts over trade more generally. A sense of how this might develop can be gained by looking at how the crisis that began in 2007 was reflected in macroeconomic policies, and in policies that could (or did) create tensions among nations.

In the aftermath of the crisis, many governments pursued economic policies that had broad macroeconomic effects; but these policies also had important external effects on commercial and other ties among nations. Both fiscal and monetary policies responded quickly to the downturn, and both raised issues directly and indirectly related to other aspects of international economic relations, creating potential externalities for other nations. Monetary policy, to take the clearest example, directly implicates the exchange rate, which in turn affects national trade relations in much the same way as import barriers or export subsidies. Stimulative monetary policies in the aftermath of the crisis pushed currencies down. If the problems had been restricted to one country or region, this might have been an appropriate response – depreciation could stimulate necessary adjustments to consumption, to real wages and to the current account. But in the context of a global crisis, attempts to weaken national currencies risk turning into a downward spiral of 'competitive devaluations', as they were called in the 1930s, and which are generally believed to have had broad negative effects on all concerned. In the years since 2008, most attention has been focused on the attempts by China, and other export-oriented developing countries, to keep their currencies weak.

The problems associated with exchange-rate policies that may impose externalities on other nations are broader than those associated with export-promoting developing countries with weak currencies. When one country's stimulative monetary policy weakens its currency, the relative strengthening of another country's currency can impede its adjustment process. These impediments can feed into broader political tensions within and among nations.

There are other ways in which issues related to the exchange rate can create political strains among nations. One such complex of problems can arise as governments attempt to sustain a fixed exchange rate. The inability to adjust the exchange rate can confront the country's tradable producers with serious competition from imports – especially if the country's inflation rate is above that of its partners, so that the currency is appreciating in real terms. It is common for governments struggling to maintain a fixed exchange rate to face strong protectionist pressures from those most affected by the added import competition. In fact, such pressures became a major political issue in Mercosur in the late 1990s. In the context of an overvalued peso associated with Argentina's currency board, Argentina faced a flood of imports: in the first eight months of 1999, Argentine imports of Brazilian textiles and footwear rose by 38% and 66% respectively. This in turn provoked protests from Argentine manufacturers, who forced the Argentine government to impose barriers on Brazilian iron, textiles and paper. The Brazilians retaliated, complained to the WTO, and even threatened to dissolve Mercosur (Carranza, 2003).

The Mercosur crisis was reminiscent of an earlier episode in the European Monetary System (EMS). The 1992/3 currency crisis in the EMS led to large devaluations of some EMS currencies. As a result, producers in countries whose currencies had been stable – in particular France and Germany – came under competitive pressures. This in turn led to domestic complaints about imports from the countries whose currencies had depreciated, which threatened the core commitments of the European Union, especially in the wake of the completion of the single European market. As Barry Eichengreen has noted about the aftermath of the 1992/3 crisis:

> The choice became whether to turn back to more freely fluctuating exchange rates, which might jeopardize the single market, or to move forward to monetary union, which would eliminate the problem of exchange rate instability by eliminating the exchange rate. Retreating to more flexible exchange rates threatened to fuel a backlash against the single market, since currency depreciation could then confer an arbitrary competitive advantage on some national producers. (Eichengreen, 2004)

As countries find themselves torn between two important concerns – to stabilise exchange rates, and to maintain the competitiveness of their tradables producers – there will be continuing possibilities that this will create conflicts among nations.

Fixed rates can also raise other difficult problems with international implications, as the adjustments they require can be severe. Some of the pain associated with the crisis in Europe was related to the exchange rate – not even considering how the very structure of the Eurozone may have contributed to the crisis. Attempts to maintain formal or informal ties to an anchor currency, especially in difficult times, can lead to major economic dislocations. For example, Estonia and Latvia endured huge drops in GDP in order to sustain their links to the euro. These sorts of painful adjustments often create a social and political backlash – they are associated with a turn towards populism in Latin America.

Fiscal policy in the crisis, too, sometimes implicated other economic relations, albeit not so directly as monetary policy. When a government undertakes stimulative fiscal policies, it is looking for effects on domestic economic activity. Yet some spending will inevitably 'leak' into demand for imports. The government of a neighbouring country might deliberately avoid otherwise appropriate fiscal expansion in the hope of being able to take advantage of the 'leaked' demand from its more fiscally active neighbour. The result could be a backlash that threatened commercial or other retaliation against the country seen to be free riding on the fiscal expansion. This concern about 'fiscal free riding' was common in the aftermath of the 2008 crisis.

We expect macroeconomic policies to continue to be the source of potential conflict, and to implicate commercial and financial relations among nations. The reasons are straightforward. In an integrated international economy, national macroeconomic policies can have immediate and powerful effects on other nations. The cross-border 'spillovers' from monetary and fiscal policies can create political tensions in other countries, and feed back into clashes among governments. This is why we have titled this chapter 'Macro is the New Trade'. In the past, many of the tensions that erupted among governments in times of economic stress took the form of trade conflicts; we think that in the future they are much more likely to take the form of conflict over macroeconomic policies.

Macroeconomic policy divergences will be intensified as the relevant actors expand to include rapidly developing countries with very different priorities and very different domestic economic structures. The monetary and fiscal policy concerns of a Turkey, Mexico, China or India differ dramatically from those of the US or the Eurozone. All of the former – and a whole host of other emerging and transitional economies – are primarily concerned with speeding their developmental paths. This often involves exchange-rate and other macroeconomic policies meant to promote exports, and not to stimulate domestic consumption. These are precisely the policies most likely to provoke controversy in the developed nations. The long-term prospect, then, is for a continuation and proliferation of conflicts analogous to the simmering USA–China dispute over the renminbi.

In this context, there are likely to be substantial conflicts over macroeconomic policy over the coming couple of decades, and significant demands for a higher level of intergovernmental collaboration. But is there really a need for purposive cooperation on international monetary policy? There is long-standing scepticism about this, for good reasons.[23] After all, most of the effects of national currency policy are felt by the nation's residents and, to the extent that one government's currency policy imposes costs on another, the target can often find a suitable response.

Nonetheless, in currency affairs as elsewhere, there are varieties of external effects that go beyond the impact on the national economy and national economic actors, and for which a unilateral response is either not possible or not desirable. Exchange rate misalignments, for example, can be the source of substantial problems for other nations and for international economic relations more generally. A government may deliberately keep its currency relatively weak, in the expectation that a depreciated currency will stimulate exports.[24] Of course, a depreciated exchange rate has a negative effect on national purchasing power, but this is solely a domestic matter in which the government has decided to trade off the welfare of exporters and import-competitors, on the one hand, for that

---

23 One classic statement is Frankel (1988); see also Eichengreen (2011).
24 It is of course understood that such policies cannot prevail forever; but there is strong evidence that the rate at which exchange rates converge towards PPP can be quite slow – certainly slow enough to allow such misalignments to have substantial effects on the real economy.

of consumers. However, a depreciated currency puts competitive pressure on the country's trading partners, and can stimulate protectionist sentiments abroad.[25] The result may be to trigger commercial discord between countries, and even to endanger broader trade agreements.

Conflicts provoked by exchange rates have placed a significant strain on the international trading system, both in bilateral relations between the countries in question, and more generally inasmuch as they have called into question the commitment of major countries to the multilateral resolution of trade disputes. Strongly misaligned currencies create problems not just for their home countries but for their economic partners, and in some instances for regional or global economic relations more generally. Intergovernmental cooperation could be of great help in avoiding some of the problems that arise as a result. And we think that such cooperation is rising higher and higher on domestic political agendas as the issues become more salient. This is especially true in the context of ongoing discussions of global macroeconomic imbalances.

7.5   Recurrent global imbalances?

It seems likely that in the absence of major policy shifts, the forces driving global macroeconomic imbalances will persist for the foreseeable future. It is hard to believe that this is a particularly good thing for the world economy. While international capital flows are a normal and natural component of an open international economy, recent experience indicates that there are reasons to be cautious about a recurrence of the kinds of global macroeconomic imbalances that led up to the Great Recession.[26]

The US is something of a special case, as its unique role allows it to continue to borrow at very low rates and in its own currency. This may of course change over time, but it is much more likely that Americans will not feel the pinch of austerity typical of a heavily-indebted country in the midst of a financial crisis. Instead, the public and private sectors will continue to be net borrowers from the rest of the world.

Nonetheless, it seems unlikely that the US will run current account deficits of the levels of the past decade, given that this would require persistence or increase of the country's large trade deficit, which would only amplify the already substantial pressures for relief from tradables industries. In addition, it would involve a continuation of sizeable Federal fiscal deficits, and these are increasingly controversial among Americans themselves. There will be domestic limits on continued deficits. There may conceivably be international limits as well, if investors abroad begin to revise their estimates of the value of US assets. This would not be due to fears of default, but rather fears of inflation. These fears are probably justified, as even reliably conservative observers have come to

---

25 Again, this is not a purely economic negative externality: the cheaper products benefit foreign consumers. The point is one of political economy: the increased demand for protection may stimulate retaliatory national policies that harm both countries.

26 Merrouche and Nier (2010) provide one sobering study.

regard several years of modest inflation as desirable to help reduce the country's debt overhang.[27] In this context, foreign appetite for dollar-denominated assets may decline, raising the costs to the US of continuing to run substantial current account and budget deficits.[28]

If the US is to reduce its deficits – a process we regard as desirable and likely – then surplus countries will need to reduce their surpluses. Yet, as our discussion has illustrated, there are substantial barriers to a meaningful reversal of the surpluses of countries that have come to rely on exports as the engine of their economic growth. The current account surpluses of both China and Japan have declined owing to the global crisis, and although the two countries' governments have indicated their desire to restrain their surpluses, there is little indication of a significant enough reorientation of economic policy in either country to point confidently in this direction over the long run. Indeed, the Japanese appear to be counting on export growth to help pull their economy forward, while the Chinese government seems bent on continuing its own emphasis on boosting manufactured exports. But this can only happen with a return to large US trade deficits, which would simply put the world back to its position before 2007. Yet in the US the conversation is largely about the opposite tack, relying on exports at least in part to fuel a more robust recovery.

In Europe, the dynamic is similar, if more troubling. There continue to be substantial current account imbalances within the Eurozone. There appears to be little indication that Germany and other northern European countries are on a path to reduce or reverse their current account surpluses with other members of the Eurozone, and of the European Union more generally. This is, of course, inconsistent with the need of peripheral European debtors to run substantial surpluses of their own in order to generate the resources necessary to service their debts. It is hard to see how the European Union will work towards a lasting resolution of its debt crisis without a major change in the pattern of trade flows between the core and the periphery. As in the relationship between the US and China, it is implausible that an intra-European rebalancing could be achieved solely by austerity in the debtors: it will almost certainly require *both* significant austerity measure in the periphery *and* stimulative measures in the core. So far, the evidence that this is likely to occur is weak.

This state of affairs implies that, left to their own devices, the world's principal centres of economic activity are on something of a macroeconomic collision course. The major debtor/deficit nations either have to or want to reduce their deficits and aim at surpluses; the major creditor/surplus nations seem bent on maintaining their surpluses. This implies, as we have indicated, that there is scope for meaningful international cooperation. Understandable attempts on the part of, say, the Spanish government to expand exports and reduce consumption are inconsistent with equally understandable attempts on the part of the German government to encourage its firms to export successfully to the Spanish market. But both goals cannot be achieved; and the world is full of countries whose policies are at odds with those of their partners.

---

27 Rogoff (2011); see also Chinn and Frieden (2012).
28 See Kitchen and Chinn (2011) for one evaluation.

This suggests that there is a real need for some coordinated effort to avoid these macroeconomic collisions, and in fact to collaborate on common policies to ease economic growth in the new post-crisis environment.[29] But is such coordination politically feasible? We think that there is greater hope for it now than there has been in recent memory. The basic principles have been discussed for the better part of a decade, as indicated in Chapter 4 above, even if the realisation of these principles has been elusive. Within the major countries, there would seem to be real opportunities to garner support for collaborative measures. Governments in the surplus countries could make the case to their publics that the goal is to increase consumption and improve national living standards. There may be opposition from entrenched export interests, but there is some scope for counteracting this with purposive measures to develop domestic markets. Most governments in the deficit countries are already constrained to undertake austerity and other adjustment measures; if cooperation is obtained, it will make these measures easier to implement. Even in the US, where the financing constraint does not bind, there appears to be real interest in everything from tax reform to entitlement restructuring.

This leads us to conclude that the G20 can make the most difference in restoring global growth and stability in the area of global macroeconomic imbalances. The Governor of the Bank of England, Mervyn King, puts the central argument best in a nutshell.

> Improved financial regulation will help intermediate the flows associated with global imbalances. But we cannot expect too much of regulation: it may well be circumvented or diluted over time, and there will be leakages, both across borders and through the shadow banking system. So the global economy will remain vulnerable to the risks associated with imbalances if they are not tackled at source. That will require some way on ensuring that countries' policies result in a sustainable outcome. ... What is needed now is a grand bargain among the major players in the world economy ... A natural forum in which to strike a bargain is the G20 ... So far, the process has failed to achieve a move to a better outcome. If we cannot achieve cooperation voluntarily then a more rules-based automatic system may need to be considered to restore global demand and to maintain future global economic and financial stability. (King, 2011)

Obviously, the Governor's analysis is not universally shared. For example, Raghuram Rajan believes that governments know what they need to do but don't do it because domestically it is politically difficult. Moreover, he argues, the value of an international grand bargain – even if this were possible – is at best uncertain. He submits that the contribution to be expected from the multilateral institutions should be a modest one, basically 'communicating the international consequences of a country's policies to that country's elite' (Rajan, 2011).

Of course, in the economics profession there is a long tradition of scepticism about the feasibility and viability of international policy coordination. Two of the most distinguished contemporary international economists, Maurice Obstfeld and Kenneth Rogoff, provided scholarly support for the sceptical view as recently

---

29   For two analyses consistent with this view see Obstfeld (2012b) and Goodhart (2012).

as a decade ago (Obstfeld and Rogoff, 2002). But that was before the great crisis, which has forced a reconsideration of what had been well-established results in the fields of macroeconomics and financial theory. Interestingly, Obstfeld and Rogoff, in a more recent collaboration, support the case for cooperation. 'The recent crisis has dramatically illustrated the important and pervasive external effects of domestic macro and financial policies. In the interest of global stability, the policy choices of sovereign nations, including their exchange rate arrangements, must be viewed as legitimate subjects for international discussion and negotiation' (Obstfeld and Rogoff, 2009).

Indeed, one of the more cogent arguments for direct attention to sustained current account imbalances comes from Obstfeld himself, in his recent Ely Lecture to the American Economics Association:

> The arguments that current account deficits are self-correcting, that huge cross-border financial flows promote efficient risk sharing, and that private-sector self interest leads to socially efficient allocations absent government-imposed distortions all look increasingly implausible in light of recent experience ... To my mind, a lesson of recent crises is that globalized financial markets present potential stability risks that we ignore at our peril. Contrary to a complete markets or 'consenting adults' view of the world, current account imbalances, while very possibly warranted by fundamentals and welcome, can also signal elevated macroeconomic and financial stresses, as was arguably the case in the mid-2000s. Historically large and persistent global imbalances deserve careful attention from policymakers, with no presumption of innocence. (Obstfeld, 2012a, pp 24, 39)

It must be admitted that as of 2012 there is no sound theory or robust empirical evidence to unwaveringly support, or reject for that matter, the case for international coordination in a world so globalised, financially and otherwise, as the present one. No model, however sophisticated, has yet captured the financial and other forms of complex connections and interdependence that exist in today's world economy. Given the recency of the phenomenon, the data to test robustly any reasonable hypothesis may not even be available in a fully satisfactory way. Ultimately, opting for or against the value of international cooperation needs to be based on good judgement informed by a mixture of theory, empirical evidence and history.

Our own judgement is that the enormous policy predicaments confronting the governments of the countries with the most significant economies – even if ultimately solving them is their own and primary responsibility—can be addressed within a framework of coordination with considerably less pain than in a scenario of mainly unilateral and inward-looking policies.

Not even the country with the biggest economy and the chief world reserve currency, the US, can be confident that unilateral policies are in its best medium- and long-term interest. It should be clear by now that minimising its own responsibility for adjustment and trying to shift as much of the burden of adjustment as possible onto others, particularly onto the large surplus countries, cannot be sustained successfully for too long. The right principle is that of symmetric responsibilities between surplus and deficit countries, not one in which just one side of the imbalance is left to fix it. If the latter were attempted stubbornly, this would invite resistance and reactions that eventually would make it more onerous for the US to achieve its own domestic policy objectives.

The idea that negotiation and agreement between only the two largest contributors to the imbalances, the US and China, would be enough to solve most of the problem should also be rejected. Not only is it the case that this approach would unnecessarily place the problem on a trajectory more prone to conflict, but there is too much at stake for others – irrespective of whether they make a large or small contribution to the imbalances—for their corresponding interests and responsibility to be ignored.

However difficult it is to achieve, there is hardly an alternative to broad consensus. It seems that the G20 accepted this principle to begin with and yet the challenge of how to obtain that consensus is proving to be an extremely recalcitrant one. On overcoming that challenge, two things are clear to us. One is that striking a grand bargain that would deliver once and for all the new architecture needed to rebalance the global economy is unfortunately not within reach any time soon – on just that part, we side more with Rajan than with King. The other is that the MAP as sketched and tried so far by the G20 is not the way to go either. The procedures to engage, define basic monitoring criteria, characterise each party's current policies, agree on each party's desirable policies and procure compliance of each party's responsibilities, as contemplated until now in the MAP, do not constitute a governance framework with any significant chance of success. The present arrangement seems to be built to provide the ones bearing the greatest responsibility for adjustment multiple escape hatches from either acknowledging or complying with that responsibility. As designed, the MAP, rather than a system of peer review, looks more like a system of peer complicity.

Safeguards, or even veto power, are usually indispensable in international agreements for reasons of political economy. But too much of any of those components is a sure formula for falling into a trap of inefficacy and irrelevance. The G20 must find a way to get out of this trap or else fail completely in its commitment to provide the cooperation needed to achieve sustainable and balanced growth.

Since a reform that fully overhauls the global financial architecture is not feasible in the near future, the G20 would do best to aim at incremental but substantive steps towards building more effective mechanisms to diagnose and address macroeconomic disequilibria which have global implications. The ultimate objective should be none other than the one determined at Pittsburgh, that of ensuring that national economic policies are mutually coherent and consistent with global stability. This implies endowing the system with effective disciplines for global adjustment. Unquestionably, this is a fundamentally multilateral endeavour that requires a truly multilateral implementation through a multilateral institution sufficiently empowered to influence national policies of both deficit and surplus countries.

In principle that institution already exists – the IMF. Although some of its articles of agreement could be interpreted so as to provide the institution with the legal capacity to play that role effectively,[30] the institution's governance, also inscribed in its articles of agreement as well as in long-standing practices, significantly limits the IMF's ability to perform that function satisfactorily. The G20 seemed to be aware of these limitations when it issued its statement of purpose for reforming the IFIs at the London summit. However, as argued before, the reforms already undertaken have fallen quite short of the original expectation and do not yet enable the IMF to perform adequately its duty of multilateral surveillance.

In order to pursue effectively its own objective of macroeconomic policy coordination, the G20 must drive a more ambitious reform to strengthen the IMF's legitimacy, governance and financial capacity. Failure to seriously reform the IMF is not due to lack of ideas about what the necessary steps are. There is already an appreciable stock of sound and responsible proposals that we endorse for the most part.[31]

Of course, the difficulty of empowering the IMF is due to some of the key players' resistance to relinquishing a portion of their long-enjoyed powers and influence. But if that resistance can be overcome, the result will be an institution that is much more effective in supporting those players' own long-term interests.

The measures necessary confront many obstacles. Domestic publics will need a great deal of convincing that their sacrifices will be worthwhile. National governments will need to be shown that their interlocutors abroad are serious. And rebalancing faces the current version of the long-standing problem of the asymmetry of the adjustment burden: there are powerful pressures on deficit countries to adjust, but surplus countries are under much less compulsion. This creates a bargaining asymmetry that can sabotage any attempt at international cooperation – as it did in the 1930s, and again as the Bretton Woods system collapsed. Nonetheless, we believe that a new push to engineer serious macroeconomic policy coordination, specifically aimed at monitoring and controlling global macroeconomic imbalances, is both desirable and possible.[32]

---

30 Article 1.6 reads: 'the purpose of the IMF (is) … to shorten the duration and lessen the degree of disequilibrium in the international balances of payments of members'. Article 4.3a reads: 'The Fund shall oversee the international monetary system in order to ensure its effective operation, and shall oversee the compliance of each member with its obligations.'

31 Examples of those ideas can be found in Eichengreen (2009); IMF Independent Evaluation Office (2008); Committee on IMF Governance Reform (2009); Palais-Royale Initiative (2011); Truman (2006).

32 One of us, Dani Rodrik, has argued that one way to bring China to the negotiating table on external imbalances would be to give the country a kind of insurance policy against the costs of too rapid an external adjustment. In principle, China's worries on job loss and social dislocation can be addressed by the use of sectoral policies (such as subsidies and other industry supports) that ease the burden of adjustment for declining industries. But WTO rules tie China's hands to a much greater extent with sectoral interventions than they do with respect to the exchange rate. A quid pro quo that is much more conducive to macroeconomic coordination would be for the US and Europe to signal that they would be willing to look the other way if China resorts to sectoral subsidies or other supports to allay social problems. From an economic standpoint, microeconomic interventions of this kind are much less costly to trade partners, and do not produce macro imbalances as long as the currency is left to adjust appropriately. For further discussion of this argument, see Rodrik (2010).

7.6   Problems of development in the new global environment

The very rapid growth of the world economy in the decade before the global financial crisis was due almost exclusively to developing countries.[33] Growth in developing countries nearly tripled from around 2% per capita in the 1980s to almost 6% before the crisis of 2008 (Figures 7.1 and 7.2). China (and the rest of developing Asia) accounts for the bulk of this performance. But growth also picked up in Latin America and Africa, starting around 1990 and reaching levels not experienced since the 1960s. Growth in the developing world was both rapid and, for once, very broadly based. The performance gap between developed and developing countries has continued to widen in the years since the onset of the crisis.

Many analysts have extrapolated that this performance will continue in decades ahead. Citigroup economists, for example, predict that per capita incomes in the world economy will grow by 3.6% in 2010–30 (very similar to the pre-crisis levels), even though each of the advanced regions of the world is projected to grow at below 2% (again, just as in the pre-2008 period) (Buiter and Rahbari, 2011, Figure 24). Subramanian estimates global growth at 3.4% over the same period, with emerging and developing countries growing at 4.6% (2011, Table 4.2). The accounting and consulting firm PwC (2011) projects China, India and Nigeria to grow at rates exceeding 4.5% until 2050. (All these estimates are in PPP and per capita terms.)

Are such growth rates in the poorer parts of the world feasible in an environment where advanced countries will be suffering from their debt hangover? Low growth in the North will imply reduced import demand, low commodity prices and uncertain capital flows. Won't such adversities bring down growth elsewhere too?

In principle, there is nothing that prevents developing countries from growing rapidly regardless of economic conditions in the advanced countries. In the medium to long term, growth depends not on demand, but on productivity increases driven by the adoption and dissemination of modern technologies. Low growth in the North does not diminish the stock of technologies that are available and which developing countries can adapt and adopt. Convergence can happen as long as developing countries follow the right policies that spur technological progress and accumulation.

---

33   This section is based on Rodrik (2011b).

Figure 7.1 Growth trends in developed and developing countries, 1950–2011

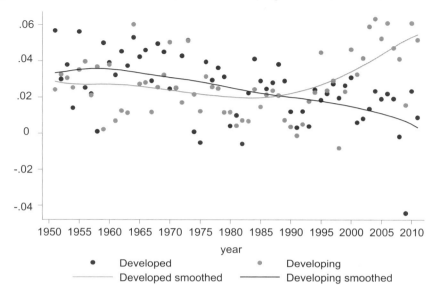

Source: A Maddison, 'Historical Statistics of the World Economy: 1–2008 AD' available at *http://www.ggdc. net/maddison/Historical_Statistics/horizontal-file_02-2010.xls*, updated with data from World Bank, World Development Indicators, and IMF, World Economic Outlook.

Figure 7.2 Developing country growth trends by region, 1950–2011

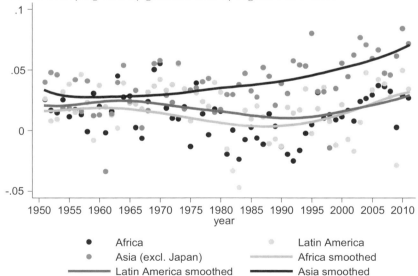

Source: As Figure 7.1.

Growth optimists point to several reasons why recent trends are likely to continue. First, there has been significant improvement in the conduct of *monetary and fiscal policies* in the developing world. With rare exceptions, macroeconomic populism has gone out of fashion. Price stability and debt sustainability have become the norm rather than the exception. Second, again with few exceptions, developing countries have opened themselves up to international trade (and to capital flows). Indeed, developing nations are now more integrated in the global economy than at any time since the 19th century. Third, developing nations are now generally much better governed. Most of Latin America is now ruled by democratically elected governments. In Africa, peace settlements have restored some semblance of stability to conflict-ridden countries such as Sierra Leone, Liberia and Côte d'Ivoire. Finally, the globalisation of markets and the spread of global production networks have created a more hospitable environment for economic catch-up, at least for countries with the necessary background conditions (so-called 'fundamentals'). These allow for the faster spread of ideas and blueprints, and facilitate the plugging of firms from poor countries into advanced technologies.

Prudent macroeconomic management, openness and improved governance surely help avoid large policy mistakes and economic disasters. By eliminating the lower tail of growth outcomes, they raise the average performance. What is less clear is whether these policy improvements in the conventional sense are sufficient – or indeed even necessary – for promoting sustained economic growth.

Countries with improved policies and institutions have been doing better of late, but it is equally true that many have yet to replicate their performance from previous eras. Brazil and Mexico, for example, are two countries that have become poster children for the new policy mindset in emerging markets. Yet these two have recently registered growth rates that are only a small fraction of what they experienced during the three decades before 1980 (Figure 7.3). And note that this cannot be explained by growth having become harder over time: these two countries had larger convergence gaps in 2000 than they did in 1950.[34] Moreover, none of the Asian growth superstars, with the possible exception of Hong Kong, fits the standard paradigm neatly. China, India and the East Asian cases are all instances of mixing the conventional and the unconventional – of combining policy orthodoxy with unorthodoxy (Rodrik, 2007, ch 1).

---

34 Neither does demography help explain the underperformance. Recent growth rates look even more disappointing, compared to the earlier period, when expressed in per worker terms.

Figure 7.3 Growth rates of GDP per capita of Brazil and Mexico by period

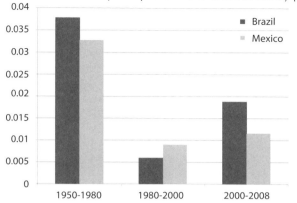

Source: World Bank, World Development Indicators.

China's policies on property rights, subsidies, finance, the exchange rate and many other areas have so flagrantly departed from the conventional rulebook that if the country were an economic basket case instead of the powerhouse that it has become, it would be almost as easy to account for it. One can make similar statements for Japan, South Korea and Taiwan during their heyday, in view of the rampant government intervention that characterised their experience. As for India, its half-hearted, messy liberalisation is hardly the example that multilateral agencies ask other developing countries to emulate.

What is common in countries that have managed to achieve sustained convergence is that they have been able to stimulate ongoing structural change from traditional, low-productivity activities to modern industries and high-value services. Evidence shows that some activities, such as organised manufacturing, are 'escalator' industries that exhibit automatic convergence to the global productivity frontier (Rodrik, 2011c). Countries that are able to latch on those industries grow rapidly while others lag behind.

The requisite structural transformation is not a process that takes place smoothly on its own, or once governments simply stabilise and liberalise. Virtually all successful countries have required pro-active policies to spawn new industries and shift resources in their direction. The mark of such policies is that they subsidise tradable sectors to compensate for government or market failures and speed up structural transformation. Trade protection, industrial policies and undervalued currencies are leading examples.

Not all countries that have experimented with these policies have succeeded, but none (again with the possible exception of Hong Kong) has experienced high growth without them. Countries that have explicitly renounced the use of these kinds of policy supports have in fact tended to experience reduced growth. The fact that Latin America's growth rate after 1990 fell considerably short of that before 1980 is intimately linked to the fact that the region began to experience *growth-reducing* structural change in the later period. Unlike in Asia or in Latin America itself before 1980, labour has been moving from higher productivity activities such as manufacturing to lower productivity ones such as informal services (Pages, 2010; McMillan and Rodrik, 2011).

The policies behind sustained convergence in Asia have been a mixture of the orthodox (macro stability, investment in human capital, emphasis on exports) with the unorthodox (undervalued currencies, industrial policies, significant state intervention). Moreover, even conventional policy objectives, such as outward orientation, have often been accomplished in unconventional ways.

Skilled reformers know that a given economic target can be achieved in diverse ways, some more unorthodox than others. Integration into the world economy can be accomplished via export subsidies (as in South Korea and Taiwan), export processing zones (as in Mauritius or Malaysia), Special Economic Zones (as in China) – or free trade (as in Hong Kong). Domestic industries can be promoted through subsidised credit (South Korea), tax incentives (Taiwan), trade protection (Brazil, Mexico and Turkey), or by reducing barriers to entry and lowering their costs of doing business. Property rights can be enhanced by importing and adapting foreign legal codes (as in Japan during the Meiji restoration) or by developing domestic variants (as in China and Vietnam). A 'messy' reform that buys off the beneficiaries of the status quo may be preferable to a 'best practice' which proves impossible to implement.

Asian-style structural transformation policies have never been easy to administer, especially outside Asia. They will face the added obstacle over the next decade of an external environment that is likely to become increasingly less permissive of their use. The WTO already has fairly strict rules against the use of export subsidies (defined somewhat broadly) and domestic content requirements – except for the poorest countries, which are exempt. But many practices have remained under the radar screen. A determined government can get an entire industry up and running by the time a WTO panel and appellate body rule on a case. We can expect this to change if industrial policies are used more widely and the rich nations continue to struggle with high unemployment and low growth. Policies that favour domestic industries will then be perceived – with some justification – as 'beggar-thy-neighbour' policies that violate the basic rules of the game and aggravate economic problems in importing countries. There will be much greater domestic political pressure to retaliate against such policies.

There are currently no international agreements against currency undervaluation, but as we discuss elsewhere in the report, the question of 'currency manipulation' has already become a flashpoint in the global economy. Unlike industrial policies which need not create macroeconomic imbalances,[35] currency undervaluation is associated with trade surpluses. That means in turn that advanced countries, as a whole, must be willing to run the counterpart trade deficits. The US, as the largest deficit country, tended to treat its external imbalance with benign neglect. The financial and economic crisis has rendered that approach more difficult to sustain. Whether driven by undervalued currencies and mercantilism or not, developing country trade surpluses will be

---

35 A production subsidy on tradables can spur the output and employment in tradables without generating a trade surplus, if the exchange rate is allowed to adjust appropriately. See Rodrik (2010b).

seen as inconsistent with the desire of industrial countries to prop up aggregate demand for their flailing economies.

No emerging country faces a bigger challenge here than China. Prior to the late 1990s, China's manufacturing industries were promoted by a wide variety of industrial policies, including high tariffs, investment incentives, export subsidies and domestic content requirements on foreign firms. As a precondition of WTO membership, China had to phase out many of these policies. From levels that were among the highest in the world as late as the early 1990s China's import tariffs fell to single-digit levels by the end of the decade. Local content requirements and export subsidies were eliminated. Currency undervaluation, or protection through the exchange rate, became the de facto substitute.

It has now become conventional wisdom, both in the West and among China's increasingly vocal economic think tanks and academics, that China has to make a transition to a different growth model, one that replaces foreign with domestic demand. However, if what matters for China's growth is ultimately the structure of production, a shift in the composition of demand may do real harm to the economy's growth. A reorientation towards services and domestic consumption would reduce the demand for its industrial products and blunt the forces of convergence described earlier. Estimates in Rodrik (2008, 2010) suggest that a 20% appreciation could reduce China's growth rate by nearly two percentage points. This is a sizeable effect, and a slowdown of this magnitude would push China dangerously close to the minimum threshold its leadership apparently believes is necessary to maintain social peace and avert social strife.

China is a special case for sure. Its leadership has been very successful since the late 1970s in tinkering with the policy regime in order to maintain the growth momentum. Perhaps it will continue to show similar ingenuity in the future. But China's case illustrates in extremis the difficulties that growth policies that promote structural transformation in the developing world will pose for underperforming industrial economies. Both because they are difficult to administer and because they will raise tensions with trade partners when successful, it is difficult to envisage that growth-promoting diversification policies will be employed en masse and effectively.

The implication is that rapid convergence will remain the exception rather than the rule in the developing world. There will be increasing tension and conflict over the nature of policies followed in those countries that are particularly successful. China will be at the forefront of this, but other large emerging market economies with unorthodox policies such as India, Brazil and Turkey will also be likely to face criticism.

One of the paradoxes of the last two decades of globalisation is that its biggest beneficiaries have been those countries that have flouted its rules – countries like China and India that have effectively played the game by Bretton Woods rather than post-1990 rules (controlled finance, controlled currencies, industrial policies, significant domestic manoeuvring room). But as such countries become large players and turn into targets for emulation, the tensions become too serious to ignore. How we handle those tensions will determine not only the future of convergence, but the future of the world economy as well.

The larger developing countries will have to take responsibility for the broad international impact of their own policies. This brings us back to macroeconomic policy, and macroeconomic imbalances. Export-oriented growth strategies have been enormously successful for many countries. But they cannot be extended to the entire world, or sustained indefinitely. Especially in the case of large, systemically important, developing countries – China, India, Brazil, perhaps a half-dozen others – governments that typically have aggressively pursued export-led growth will now have to take into account the global impact of their national policies. This will require concessions on both sides, and will run up against powerful interests in both sets of countries. However, the most likely alternative is a strong backlash in the developed countries against the macroeconomic and trade policies of the developing nations, a backlash whose impact would be harmful to both sides.

8 Looking Ahead

Contemporary international economic integration has been a powerful force for economic growth and development. In broad historical terms, the most striking development of the past 30 years has been very rapid growth in Asia, which has helped lift hundreds of millions of people above the absolute poverty line. This feat would almost certainly have been impossible if these nations had not had access to the world's markets, capital and technologies. Even if only on these grounds, current levels of economic integration are of value and worth sustaining.

The global reach of today's markets has led many to call for expanded 'global governance', to provide some of the typical functions of government at the international level. The argument implies that global markets require global regulation and management. Certainly there are many circumstances in which national governments, acting separately, cannot adequately deal with the problems that arise with flows of goods, capital and people across borders. The maintenance of an open international economy requires substantive and purposive cooperation among the major economic powers.

However, international cooperation is difficult enough in normal times, untroubled by crises or new entrants. National publics focus on national concerns, and are often loth to see their representatives deal away national prerogatives on behalf of vague promises of eventual global gains. National policymakers cannot ignore the reservations of their constituents, and may be tightly constrained in how much they can do and how far they can go in making international commitments.

These are not normal times. The global crisis that began in 2007 continues to trouble the world economy, some of its constituent parts more than others. Europe has fallen into a second recessionary dip, driven by the continued difficulties associated with its debt overhang. The recovery in the US is halting, and job growth in particular continues to be disappointing. Virtually all developed countries face medium- and long-term fiscal challenges, some more dramatic than others. To complicate matters, there are a number of important new emerging-economy players on the world scene, and their priorities and preferences are quite different from those of the traditional incumbents. All this raises major questions about the future of international economic cooperation.

Economic hard times, an increase in the number of major actors, and growing divergences in preferences will complicate the negotiation and implementation of major new global measures. For this reason, we think it the better part of valour for the principal governments to focus their attention on areas in which cooperation is particularly desirable, and in which it is particularly likely to be successful. We draw on both normative theory, and an evaluation of the domestic economic and political circumstances of the major actors, to suggest what the principal goals should be, and where the principal obstacles may lie.

We anticipate that the most important issues of the next decade or so are likely to revolve around global macroeconomic problems. It appears likely that there will be a continuation or resurgence of the global current account imbalances that were important contributors to the crisis. There are important domestic pressures in the surplus, creditor, countries that will make it hard for them to shift gears to consume more and save less, import more and export less. There are analogous domestic pressures in the deficit, debtor, countries to resist the austerity measures necessary to turn their own finances around. We reject the notion that one nation's difficulties in adjusting to new financial conditions are only of interest to that one nation. We have experienced the serious consequences of uncoordinated macroeconomic policies leading to major capital flow cycles and attendant booms and busts. It is hard to believe that a recurrence of large-scale imbalances will somehow be more benign in the future than they have been in the past, or in the present. For this reason, we anticipate (and endorse) substantial efforts to coordinate macroeconomic policies to avoid a recurrence of the past crisis. Although enhanced cooperation on international trade and international financial regulation might be useful, we do not see it as so necessary, or so likely to be achieved, as cooperation on macroeconomic policies.

Excessive macroeconomic imbalances, and the policies that produce them, can impose serious costs on other nations: benefits they may generate to the home country comes at the expense of risks, and losses, to others. This provides a strong normative argument for coordination to address such imbalances. Although the problem goes beyond currency manipulation, mercantilist currency policies are a specific and significant example of the problem. So too is the fact that these imbalances are historically a major source of protectionist outbursts. It is *not* the case that global macroeconomic imbalances were the only cause of the crisis, or that they are the only source of concern in the world economy. However, we regard macroeconomic policy as the area where the potential gains from coordination are largest.

Macroeconomic policy differences are likely to be at the core of international economic problems for the foreseeable future. Little has been accomplished to avoid serious disagreements among the principal developed and emerging-market governments. Domestic political obstacles in every major country, and the difficulties of negotiating agreement among governments with very different views, stand in the way of progress on this front. Nonetheless, we believe that movement to better coordinate national macroeconomic policies, and in particular to avoid a resurgence of global current account imbalances, is both desirable and feasible.

Discussions and Roundtables

Part I: Formal discussion of Chapters 1 to 4

Benoît Coeuré, *Member of the Executive Board, European Central Bank, Frankfurt am Main*

Benoît Coeuré agreed that the future of global cooperation is a pressing issue as the environment of globalisation has changed during the financial crisis. He acknowledged the importance of the topic for central bankers and admitted that he was pleased with the authors' conclusion that cooperation between central banks has proven to work reasonably well in comparison with international political cooperation during the crisis years. Today's degree of international stability is due mainly to monetary policy, he said. But there is a caveat: central banks aren't concerned only with monetary policy, they also increasingly care about financial stability, and it will be seen over time whether they can achieve the same degree of cooperation in that field.

Benoît Coeuré gave the report credit for dealing with the issue of global imbalances so extensively. He observed that a rebalancing of current accounts within the Eurozone was in the focus of the ECB. He structured the rest of his commentary into four parts.

First, he highlighted the difference between cooperation on technical issues – like the harmonisation of technical standards – on the one hand and broader political cooperation on the other hand. It is political cooperation, Benoît Coeuré said, that incorporates potential for conflict in global cooperation. He underlined the importance of distinguishing between these two areas of cooperation in order to clearly identify which institutions are better prepared to deal with these issues. For example, the WTO is best suited to handle technical issues, but more politically sensitive questions belong to political leaders. The recent trend has been towards discussing more and more technical issues at the highest political level, which has led to a politicisation of issues which previously remained at the technical level. An example is the discussion about non-tariff barriers to trade that is high on the Doha Development Agenda. Liberalising the service sector or government procurement is politically too loaded to be dealt with by technical agencies. Another example is the financial transaction tax now being discussed by the G20. Unfortunately, the politicisation of technical issues is making global cooperation more difficult.

Second, the success – or failure – of global cooperation hinges on the distinction between policies aimed at creating new rules and what Peter Kenen called regime-preserving cooperation. Regime preservation is easier to agree on at the international level than new common policy standards and regulations. This is one reason why it is so hard for the G20 to make meaningful decisions. The policy reforms discussed by the G20 concern areas in which governments have strong national interests and they are thus unlikely to be agreed upon within the context of the G20, except in exceptional circumstances.

Third, extending the G7 to the G20 is a response to the need to include new actors in the decision-making process at the global level. Benoît Coeuré praised the report's extensive treatment of this aspect. However, he warned against some negative consequences of this ongoing process for global decision-making: including more actors means creating a greater heterogeneity of preferences (especially as the new actors' preferences diverge decisively from those of the old actors), which makes reaching an agreement more difficult. The gains from including more actors in the decision-making process may thus be outweighed by the losses in capacity to act. This may explain why it has proven easier to agree on financial regulation, where the preferences of developed and emerging economies do not differ substantially, than on climate change, for which the United Nations has accepted 'common but differentiated responsibility'.

Finally, Benoît Coeuré mentioned the lack of intellectual consensus on what form global cooperation should take. This is because of increased complexity and uncertainty in the economic system: as an example, there is a huge divergence of opinions on how the financial crisis was brought about. In addition, the crisis and the rise of emerging market economies have together eroded the West's ideological hegemony, in the Gramscian sense. In order to make political cooperation more efficient, it is worth considering rebuilding intellectual consensus within a broader set of nations, he concluded.

Rajiv Kumar, *Secretary General, Federation of Indian Chambers of Commerce and Industry, New Delhi*
Rajiv Kumar praised the insights that the report contained, even though he would have liked to see a case study on India as well. Addressing the role of the G20, he recalled that its origin lies in the Asian financial crisis and in the subsequent need for an arena that includes emerging economies for discussing international financial issues. Only later has the agenda been extended to include global policy and development issues. The problem of the G20 is its lack of legitimacy and efficiency. Concerning legitimacy, most global issues are dealt with already by other bodies: global financial sector regulation takes place within the BIS and trade regulation within the WTO, while most macroeconomic issues such as global imbalances or the euro crisis are considered genuinely domestic (or inner-EU) problems that require domestic solutions. Is the G20 still legitimate? Rajiv Kumar gave two reasons for answering this question in the affirmative: first, the G20 is needed to create support for globalisation, which is currently eroding; second, the G20 can contribute to making the Doha Round successful, for

example by creating consensus against protectionism or for including agriculture in the agenda.

Rajiv Kumar then addressed the question of global governance in a post-hegemonic world. He expressed the opinion that the US should not yet be written off as leader in the global arena. No other state is able to take over that role. Instead of discussing hegemony, the focus should be on how to bring together two different types of capitalism, the Western model and the Chinese and Singapore type. In this regard, Rajiv Kumar put forward two suggestions. First, it is important to make China an equal player in international cooperation. Therefore a new type of G8 is needed. This body should not be as wide as the G20, however; it will be sufficient just to include China in the G8. Second, the role of the IMF should be strengthened. The IMF demonstrated its expertise when it cautioned against financial imbalances as early as in 2007. It should be given real autonomy as an advisory body on macroeconomic issues.

Yung Chul Park, *Professor, Division of International Studies, Korea University, Seoul*
Yung Chul Park acknowledged that the report was an excellent study that has provided him with many new insights. It helped him better understand the problems connected with constructing a new economic order while at the same time drawing attention to the persistence of global imbalances which might presage a new crisis. He then highlighted six issues.

First, the current crisis is not only a crisis of the global financial system and of the real economy. It is equally a crisis of capitalism. In many emerging markets, market liberalisation is being put at risk.

Second, the crisis has eroded the credibility of the economic profession. Economists have proven unable either to foresee the crisis or to agree on its cures. Therefore, economists will not be able to contribute to the construction of a new economic order.

Third, Yung Chul Park asked whether the construction of a new economic order can be achieved within the current political framework. Considering the two major players, the US and China, it is clear that the USA does not want to see its political role diminished, while at the same time China will not accept a new order that requires reconsidering the role of its monetary policy as long as it is not acknowledged as a new leader in the international sphere.

Fourth, the issue of global imbalances remains unsolved and it cannot be assumed that it will be resolved in the near future. Global imbalances have been top of the agenda in international negotiations, but global leaders are currently losing interest in further negotiating the issue. Apart from continuing international talks, Yung Chul Park called for more scientific evidence on the topic. It is crucial to detect what lies in the heart of global imbalances. He mentioned China's exchange rate policy in this context.

Fifth, Yung Chul Park talked about the role of emerging economies in global cooperation. He warned that they could turn into stumbling blocks for a multilateral agreement. As many of them (like Korea) were not invited to contribute to the construction of a new economic order, they might in the long run prefer bilateral or plurilateral free trade agreements that help them protect their export markets to a joint international agreement with the developed world.

Sixth, many emerging economies are unsure about which exchange rate regime to adopt.

Seventh, most emerging countries have the political objective of running small current account surpluses because, for them, foreign reserves serve as insurance and indicate to foreign lenders and investors the soundness of monetary policy.

Finally, Yung Chul Park expressed scepticism about the role foreseen by the authors of the report for the G20 and the IMF. While the bigger countries are losing interest in the G20, Korea's ideas are not listened to in this body. The USA does not have any interest in cooperating within the G20 because it is internationally predominant in terms of monetary policy and financial regulation. China, on the other hand, does not want to have the renminbi on the G20 agenda; for China, this is an issue to be discussed bilaterally with the USA. The European Union countries on the other hand are reluctant to discuss problems connected to the euro. So all in all, the most pressing global economic questions are not on the agenda of the G20. He observed instead a trend towards concentrating on long-term structural economic issues in the G20. He also believed that the IMF is unlikely to be an important cornerstone of future international cooperation.

Takatoshi Ito, *Professor, Graduate School of Economics, University of Tokyo, Tokyo*
Takatoshi Ito started by addressing the question raised by the authors: why did economic recovery proceed so slowly after the crisis? In his opinion, this crisis has simply not been deep enough to allow for a fast recovery.

He expressed doubts as to whether global imbalances were the major cause of the global financial crisis. Instead, he pointed to lax financial supervision in the USA and UK and to the lack of effectiveness of financial authorities prior to 2007. By contrast, financial surpluses and deficits are an integral part of an integrated world economy and therefore nothing to be concerned about.

Concerning the euro crisis, Takatoshi Ito asked if the authors considered it to be a solvency or a liquidity crisis. He asked whether a lender of last resort would help Greece solve its crisis, and whether Spain and Italy had only become affected by the Greek crisis because liquidity had not been provided to Greece in a timely way. At the same time, the euro crisis could also be seen as a window of opportunity for structural reforms in the Eurozone. This kind of effect was observed during the Asian crisis where IMF intervention and domestic reform policies led to major restructurings of inefficient economies.

He also felt that the authors did not focus enough on Asia. India, in particular, but also other Asian countries have turned into centres of growth and therefore need to be included in any future architecture of global cooperation. These countries are becoming more and more confident; they protect themselves by piling up foreign reserves and embrace inclusive and sustainable growth. The question to be asked is whether this increase in confidence will have a positive or negative effect on global cooperation.

Discussing the existing pillars of global cooperation, he wondered whether the IMF, the World Bank and the WTO should be revived or replaced. These bodies are too centred on the euro and the USA to leave adequate room for the interests of emerging Asia. Many Asian countries still view the IMF critically because of its advice during the Asian crisis. Now these countries are closely scrutinising the stance taken by the IMF towards the euro crisis countries and will assess its credibility accordingly. Takatoshi Ito mentioned that with the Doha Round deadlocked and free trade agreements proliferating, the WTO is also not a powerful body at the moment. However, the G20 is unable to replace the WTO and IMF. First, it lacks a legal basis; second, it is too big to act effectively; third it does not have its own secretary but depends on the IMF in this regard – which naturally makes it dependent on the IMF. That is why Takatoshi Ito considered a fundamental reform of the IMF and the WTO as more promising than expanding and upgrading the G20.

To conclude, Takatoshi Ito probed whether international cooperation is needed at all. From the viewpoint of game theory, cooperation is needed to assure that in the case of multiple Nash equilibria, the equilibrium that gives the higher pay-off is obtained. In practice, however, things aren't that simple. Most important, China's scepticism towards global cooperation has to be overcome. One way of achieving this would be to give China the position of managing director in the IMF.

Part II: General discussion of Chapters 1 to 4

Richard Portes, *Professor of Economics, London Business School and CEPR*
For Richard Portes it is important to focus on domestic politics prior to the financial crisis in order to explain global imbalances. For example, differences in unit labour costs have led to prices differences between tradable and non-tradable goods. He stressed also that there is no consensus between economists that the renminbi is undervalued.

Michael Pettis, *Senior Associate, Carnegie Endowment, Beijing*
Michael Pettis argued that it is important to look for the reason why China appreciated its currency in the last years. The ensuing adjustment operated mostly through lower investment rates and less through lower savings rates, as would have been desirable. These developments are not sustainable and have not changed anything about the fact that the renminbi is undervalued. The authors of the report remain of the opinion that China should appreciate its currency.

Cédric Tille, *Professor of International Economics, Graduate Institute of International and Development Studies, Geneva*
Cédric Tille emphasised the economic reasons for global coordination and went on to call for further discussions about regional cooperation. As an example he mentioned the banking sector in the Eurozone, where regulation is not absolutely obliged to be global but could be regional in nature. On the issue of global imbalances, Cédric Tille highlighted the difference between gross and net imbalances. Net imbalances are the ones that matter in discussing the causes of

the crisis, but while gross capital flows between banks exploded prior to the crisis, net flows stayed more or less unchanged. Therefore, in looking for causes of the crisis, it is important to take into account models which show how financial shocks are transmitted to the real sphere without net global imbalances.

Alexander Swoboda, *Professor of Economics Emeritus, Graduate Institute of International and Development Studies, Geneva*
Global imbalances are symptoms rather than the cause of the financial crisis, Alexander Swoboda stated. There are 'good' and 'bad' imbalances—the latter reflecting various types of distortions, notably inappropriate policies. At the heart of contemporary 'bad' current account imbalances lie distortions in national saving and investment, in particular unsustainable fiscal policies; so it is the government budgets that need to be readjusted in the first place in order to correct such imbalances However, it is often not in the interest of national politicians to correct imbalances because of the political constraints that they are facing.

On a global level, what has to be done to avoid repeating the mistakes of the past is well known; it includes limiting the pro-cyclical character of financial regulation, to ensure market discipline by regulation that is enforceable and to create some basic, universally recognised code of conduct for external adjustment policies under various exchange rate regimes. The Washington and Toronto declarations of the G20 have not always proven helpful in this regard because they focus too strongly on technicalities and not enough on political feasibility.

Dani Rodrik, *Rafiq Hariri Professor of International Political Economy, Harvard University, Cambridge*
Dani Rodrik acknowledged that it is crucial to find an appropriate level of international cooperation which allows national politicians to extract positive externalities from foreign governments' policies. Domains for global cooperation should be those where cooperation is in the domestic interest of each country.

Ulrich Kohli, *Professor of Economics, University of Geneva*
Ulrich Kohli reiterated a sceptical view on the importance of global imbalances as a cause of the crisis. Instead, he referred to low central bank interest rates that had made money cheap and created housing bubbles that eventually burst. In this light, it isn't surprising that the real economy recovered slowly in the USA: the private sector needs time to correct its borrowing behaviour.

Amlan Roy, *Managing Director, Head of Global Demographic and Pensions Fixed Income Research Department, Crédit Suisse, London*
Amlan Roy highlighted the link between global imbalances and demographic change. Referring to Huntington's *Clash of Civilizations*, he stated that demographic change requires international political coordination and that the demographic power of China should be worked out more in the report. He also made mention of the book *Coordination Games* by Russell Cooper and the theory

of same name which lays out the analytical framework for macro-coordination and complementarities.

Luigi Buttiglione, *Head of Global Strategy, Brevan Howard Investment Products, Geneva*

Luigi Buttiglione stated that the recovery of output growth in the USA is not only of concern to the country itself, but also to the rest of the world and in particular to China, because China fears an economic downturn in its domestic economy. Global coordination can be a way to offset these developments.

Jean-Pierre Danthine, *Vice-Chairman of the Governing Board, Swiss National Bank, Zurich*

Jean-Pierre Danthine also expressed scepticism concerning the role of high current account imbalances in Europe. He stated that the domestic policies that lie at the heart of high imbalances are indeed a source of externalities. Germany's structural reforms that were intended to enhance competitiveness of the national economy could create negative spillovers in other euro countries. But there is no economic justification for preventing such adjustments.

Dani Rodrik, *Rafiq Hariri Professor of International Political Economy, Harvard University, Cambridge*

Dani Rodrik agreed that global coordination could set benchmarks for structural reforms that would offset negative externalities. For example, a unilateral lowering of import taxes creates externalities for competitor countries that are usually taken into consideration by domestic politicians.

Claudio Borio, *Deputy Head Monetary and Economic Department, Director of Research and Statistics, Bank for International Settlements, Basel*

Claudio Borio said that credit booms are not necessarily linked to in current account deficits. Some of the most disruptive credit booms in history (Japan in the 1980s, the US in the 1920's) occurred in countries with large current account surpluses. The credit boom that triggered the US crisis was largely financed domestically. To the extent that it was financed across borders, the financing had mainly come from regions that were in balance (Eurozone) or in deficit (UK). There had also been a lot of round tripping. Finally, to understand the nature of the strains it was also important to look at the consolidated balance sheets of banks, considering them as a unit irrespective of the location of their operations. In particular, the foreign banks that were active in the US were mostly British or continental European, not Asian.

He noted that monetary and exchange rate policies are not discussed in the report. Yet, the countries most affected by the financial crisis have set the interest rate effectively at zero in order to boost aggregate demand. Countries in the periphery that try to resist appreciation must either keep interest rates low or intervene in the foreign exchange market and invest in advanced countries. In this way, credit and asset price booms are already becoming a problem again in the periphery, as unusually accommodative monetary policy stance is generalised across the world.

Jeffry Frieden, *Professor of Government, Harvard University, Cambridge*
Jeffry Frieden agreed that exchange rate policy is another area where global cooperation would be desirable, for example in order to avoid trade disputes. The uncoordinated exchange rate policies of the 1930s contributed to financial anarchy. However, it is important to identify where cooperation is not only desirable, but also feasible.

Michael Pettis, *Senior Associate, Carnegie Endowment, Beijing*
Michael Pettis acknowledged that it is not just large current account deficits but imbalances in general that cause problems for the international economy. At the root of unbalanced current accounts lie domestic policies that are distorting savings rates: in the USA, the savings rate was pushed down by money creation used to finance the Iraq war, while on the other hand in Germany and China policies aimed at depressing domestic household consumption triggered high savings rates.

Part III: Formal discussion of Chapters 5 to 7

José Antonio Ocampo, *Professor, School of International and Public Affairs and Member of the Committee on Global Thought, Columbia University, New York*
José Antonio Ocampo dealt with three major issues: the institutional setting, global social and economic interactions, and the report's conclusion that cooperation is more promising in macroeconomic than in other areas.

Concerning the institutional setting, he argued that what should matter for good international governance are well-functioning treaty-based organisations. These organisations have the advantage that they are accountable to their member states and that they have independent secretariats. The latter are particularly important as they guarantee follow-up of the mandates and decisions, and to the balance between large and small members. On the other hand, unlike the IMF, which is a fairly universal organisation, the G20 is not representative. Furthermore, the G20 duplicates mandates that the first article of the IMF Agreement gives to that organisation.

Ocampo then observed that three main aspects drive international cooperation: managing interdependence, reduction of international inequalities, and dissemination of global standards. While the report mainly focuses on interdependence of domestic policies, Ocampo argued that international cooperation was largely about standards. He gave the example of the labour standards which have been set by the International Labour Organization since the 1920s, and the economic, social and environmental standards agreed in the United Nations in the postwar period. He indicated that the report's typology of international cooperation focuses exclusively on economic issues.

Ocampo agreed, in any case, with the authors' emphasis on macroeconomic cooperation as the central issue, both currently and in the years to come. He observed, however, that a major problem in this regard is that emerging markets are deeply divided on macroeconomic cooperation. More broadly, they tend to disagree on many other concerns, as reflected in the common divergence of views between China and India on many global issues. Because the major emerging powers are unable to seek a common agenda, the Western coalition is likely to remain dominant.

He further pointed out that the report does not give enough attention to South–South trade flows, even though these flows have become increasingly important. These flows have important implications especially for developing countries. Since wage income is rising in China, other developing countries will be able to become exporters of low-skilled manufacturing goods. Moreover, China increasingly imports primary goods from African and Latin American countries and devotes its resources to the export of manufactured goods. In this sense, China is at the centre of a new core–periphery system that constitutes an important part of South–South trade.

On a minor note, Ocampo objected to the report's characterisation of Brazil's recent growth performance as having been driven by improvements in the terms of trade. In his view, it has been determined by the dynamism of the domestic market, which has benefited in turn from improvements in income distribution.

Jonas Pontusson, *Professor of Political Science, University of Geneva*
Jonas Pontusson expressed his admiration for the report's balance between pessimism and optimism. He also strongly liked the focus on the interaction between domestic politics and international politics. Noting that governments need to cooperate in some fields but that their ability to do so depends on their domestic constituents, he asked two questions: who are these constituents and what do they need in order to cooperate? Pontusson disagreed with the authors' conclusions that governments want to cooperate and that public opinion acts as a severe constraint. In his view, it is special interest politics that matters instead. The report also misses a discussion of state actors and unelected elites which also pursue their own particular interests.

Pontusson then presented some public opinion data which confirm growing scepticism towards globalisation within developed countries. However, further insights are available. Despite the current financial crises, free trade is not seen as bad, which matches the limited trend towards protectionist policies, so far at least. He believed that this was not only due to governmental resistance to protectionist policies but rather to the absence of political pressure, which stands in sharp contrast to the 1970s.

He next addressed the report's suggestion that governments can only focus either on international cooperation or on domestic problems. This 'limited attention span' theory, which he viewed as an American centred view, as well as the proposition that governments have been stepping back from international cooperation since the beginning of the crises need more evidence in order to be convincing. He formulated the alternative hypothesis that international governance reforms become possible when governments are unable to solve their domestic problems.

Pontusson wondered whether beggar-thy-neighbour or beggar-thyself policies were at the origin of the global imbalances. Domestically, different interest groups call for different sets of policies with diverging distributional implications. The key analytical challenge is to build a linkage between the domestic distributive conflict and the distributive conflict across countries at the international level. For instance, popular resistance to external deficit reduction is seen as natural, yet the interesting question is what the obstacles are to surplus reduction. He was particularly puzzled by the description of China in the report. It is not clear whether the adjustment requested from China can be considered good or bad once we take into account the negative reaction of the population to lower economic growth.

Pontusson also discussed inequality with a particular focus on the USA. He agreed with the report that rising inequality fed into rising anti-globalisation sentiments. If the adjustment of the US deficit translated into reduced public expenditure, this could fuel further inequality and might as well be counterproductive. More generally, he argued, we should be worried about the redistributive implications of austerity programmes within and across countries.

To conclude, Pontusson highlighted the difference between global imbalances within the Eurozone and global imbalances in the rest of the world. In the world economy, the surplus countries are the poor countries, while in the Eurozone the rich countries are the surplus countries. This suggests that the correction of imbalances is more feasible within the Eurozone.

Christian Kastrop, *Deputy Director General, Bundesministerium der Finanzen, Berlin*
Christian Kastrop expressed strong appreciation for the report. His analysis focused on Europe and more particularly on Germany. He stated that governments only comply with their international obligations if they are consistent with domestic interests. He acknowledged that the report goes beyond a purely economic perspective to consider also the political economy aspects, which are important in countries as diverse as Germany and Greece.

He noted that the increase in spreads within the Eurozone can be largely attributed to the loss of credibility of European institutions. He acknowledged that Europe's governance had some weaknesses prior to the crises, which caused a lack of credibility in the no-bailout clause and a moral hazard situation. Economic and political coordination is also deficient. On the one side, current agreements overestimate fiscal policy coordination, while on the other side they underestimate current account imbalances, competitiveness aspects and the development of financial markets.

Kastrop commented on some solutions that would facilitate international cooperation. A first solution would be a centralised organ. This would reduce coordination problems but it would require much stronger democratic legitimisation and would therefore not be very plausible. The opposite solution could be a decentralised decision-making process externally controlled by the Commission, checking the consistency of domestic policies with long-run growth. This solution does not appear very feasible either because it would require a loss of sovereignty. The heterogeneity of the EU member countries is already accommodated through an enhanced federalism and the subsidiary principle; however, convincing policy coordination is necessary.

Any alternative solution must combine an incentive-driven enforceable mechanism and a crisis resolution mechanism. The risk is to envisage mechanisms as remedies to crises without paying attention to their preventive capacities and thus without a long-term focus. It is equally important that the mechanisms are sufficient in size and, above all, that they can be implemented. This is why, Kastrop argued, further structural and competitiveness reforms will be necessary in order to calm the markets. He further strongly agreed with the authors that a comprehensive financial regulation framework in Europe is necessary. Yet the European heterogeneity of views may impede this as some countries are interested in protecting their markets.

Kastrop listed a couple of questions that remain open. What if a country continuously fails to deliver on its proposed reforms? Is the crisis prevention mechanism big enough for certain countries? In his view, every solution must be market-driven because market spreads are an important early warning system.

Xin Wang, *Secretary General, China Society for International Economic Relations*
Xin Wang concentrated his comments on two topics: domestic political constraints for international cooperation, and China's role in global imbalances. He acknowledged the excellent work done by the report in explaining the domestic political constraints for international governance. Regarding China, the report mainly focuses on its development model. Wang asked how far China is involved in participating in international governance and whether this involvement is consistent with its development stage.

He saw China as increasingly more active in global governance. At the same time, the Chinese public may not welcome deeper involvement if it is costly, because China is still a poor country. Furthermore, Chinese elites are suspicious of the current international system because it is dominated by the Western countries. Wang attributed this reticence to China's long history of being invaded by foreign powers.

Wang recognised that, even though the imbalance between the USA and China has recently weakened, global imbalances remain a big issue. This has led the Chinese government to reassess its economic development model and to rely less on net exports. He observed that the Chinese current account surplus has decreased substantially not only because of weaker external demand but mainly as a result of domestic structural changes. For instance, Chinese wages are showing a strong increase, which accelerates domestic consumption. With further reforms of the development model, Wang expects that there will be further improvements in China's current account.

Wang agreed with previous speakers that Europe's internal imbalances are more worrying than the global imbalances, with far-reaching implications. The China–USA imbalance is sustainable for some time, because the financial and economic linkages are very strong and because China continues to finance the imbalance, even if this is not necessarily healthy for China. In Europe, on the other hand, the surplus countries finance the deficit countries at a time when the linkage between them is becoming weaker and weaker. The question then is which international mechanism is the best for discussion of these internal imbalances, especially considering that power has shifted from Brussels to domestic capitals. Wang believed that this had to be discussed as it has important implications for the global economy.

Part IV: General discussion of Chapters 5 to 7

Edmond Alphandéry, *Chairman, CNP Assurances, Paris*
Edmond Alphandéry appreciated the extraordinary quality of the report. His first remark concerned the current euro crises. He agreed with the statement that deficits can be desirable if they are used for productive investments. Consequently, there are two types of current account deficits, good ones and bad ones. Good current account deficits promise economic growth, while bad current account deficits only drive up debt levels. This is why domestic demand has to be broken down into non-productive and productive demand. A trade imbalance driven by non-productive demand may destabilise the economy. The Eurozone has been entirely focused on the fiscal side, which did not represent an issue for Spain before the crisis. As a consequence, Alphandéry suggested the introduction of a new indicator measuring excessive non-productive aggregate demand. Fiscal restraints continue to be necessary but only to restrain excessive non-productive aggregate demand. The proposed indicator would be useful in assessing the current deficits in the European periphery.

Alphandéry's second remark referred to the Chinese development model. He saw the origin of the Chinese current account surplus, which is at the heart of the current global imbalances, as the outcome of a huge price distortion. Wages, interest rates and the exchange rate are too low. The beneficiary of this model is the Chinese productive sector at the expense of Chinese households and of foreign partners. Alphandéry estimated that the current account surplus would disappear and eventually turn into deficit if the Chinese government allowed these prices to coincide with their fundamental levels.

The idea could well be extended to all countries. Allowing equilibrium prices to prevail would most likely allow the global economy to be far more balanced in the long term. Macroeconomic cooperation would not really be necessary, except for an enforcement mechanism that would ensure that countries actually comply. The gold standard constituted such a situation in the past.

Jeffry Frieden, *Professor of Government, Harvard University, Cambridge*
Jeffry Frieden responded to Pontusson's statement on domestic constituencies. While looking at public opinion data to examine domestic constraints, the report does not ignore the role of powerful special interests. It is simply that public opinion data is more readily available and can be used to illustrate the importance of domestic constraints. He noted that while public opinion data indeed show

that most people think that trade is good for the country, they also view trade as bad for them personally. He agreed with Pontusson's view that public opinion is not the main obstacle to international cooperation but that powerful special interests are. This is clearly true in the case of financial regulations, monetary policy and other kinds of regulatory policies, as well as in the case of China's development strategy.

Dani Rodrik, *Rafiq Hariri Professor of International Political Economy, Harvard University, Cambridge*
Dani Rodrik concentrated his comments on the importance of current accounts. He invited the audience to imagine a world in which current accounts did not matter, since markets were perfectly integrated, both economically and institutionally. An example would be the US, in which the current account deficit of Florida with respect to the rest of the country is probably way higher than the Greek or Spanish deficit. This does not constitute any problem since Florida is fully integrated in the US. Simply bad decisions will only translate into bad consequences for those that took those bad decisions. In the Eurozone, on the other hand, it spills over into sovereign risk and on other lenders. Internal balances should not matter inasmuch as the Eurozone is financially integrated. The problem arises because of the lack of institutional and political integration. Unless the Eurozone adopts some form of integration such as in the USA, it must find ways of handling current account imbalances, but in Europe as elsewhere in the world current account imbalances are essentially unsustainable.

Michael Pettis, *Senior Associate, Carnegie Endowment, Beijing*
Michael Pettis addressed the good versus bad deficit issue. To that effect, he imagined a two-country world, namely Germany and Spain. A good trade imbalance would occur if Spanish investment levels were rising very quickly due to growth opportunities or due to a sharp increase in productivity. In that case, Spanish investment levels would exceed its savings rate, translating into capital flows from Germany and causing a current account deficit for Spain. A bad deficit could occur as the result of distortions in the German economy that forced up its savings rate, for instance policies that reduced consumption as share of GDP through household income reductions. Germany's net exports of capital to Spain would then cause two reactions in Spain. The investment rate could go up or the savings rate could go down. The rise in Spanish investment could be due to an increase in Spanish private, productive investment; this is not very likely if the increased Spanish demand is absorbed by the German tradable-goods sector, which would instead reduce investment in Spain. Alternatively, the government could carry out the additional investment. If either investment does not increase while German capital is imported, then by definition the Spanish savings rate has to go down. This could be done through an independent central bank, driving down interest rates. Since Spain did not have this option, the logical consequence was the consumption and real estate boom financed by household debts. This analysis explains that what happened in Spain was just the logic of the balance of payments. In his opinion, Spain can only decide between higher

debt or unemployment. A better solution lies in a reversal of Germany's current account.

Richard Portes, *Professor of Economics, London Business School and President of CEPR*
Richard Portes strongly disagreed with the report's statement that stronger democratic accountability of national parliaments might reduce the influence of the banking industry. In the US it is just the other way around, due to successful lobbying by the banking sector, which has a huge effect on financial regulation. In that sense, democratic accountability is not necessarily good. Portes went on to argue that, as opposed to what is stated in the report, there is broad support for harmonising financial regulation in Europe with the exception of the UK. The broad support is attributed to the politicians' desire to level the playing field.

Portes also criticised the report regarding its view on currency wars. He disagreed that the US dollar has proven relatively strong since 2008. Actually, the US dollar has depreciated and the USA is therefore winning the currency wars, a fact other countries are complaining about.

Finally Portes addressed the coordination failure problem often mentioned in the report. Coordination of actions may be in the interest of deficit countries but surplus countries may not feel attracted to it. The goal must be to educate policymakers in surplus countries by showing them that it may be in their interest to act. The case of China and the USA during the past decade is exemplary. The USA was neither able to generate more external demand nor to consolidate its fiscal side, and therefore ended up with quantitative easing. Chinese policymakers did not properly understand this US inability. Understanding these linkages is necessary if we can ever hope to overcome coordination failures.

Alexander Swoboda, *Professor of Economics Emeritus, Graduate Institute of International and Development Studies, Geneva*
Alexander Swoboda did not agree with the statement that China acts to the detriment of its foreign partners. China mainly acts to its own detriment, giving subsidies to the rest of the world by transferring resources at the expense of its own population. He agreed with Portes that the important point is to convince China to change its behaviour.

Regarding the Spain-Germany example offered by Pettis, Swoboda suggested that the example could easily be translated to the China-USA relationship to conclude that China forces the US into a trade deficit. But more importantly, he wished to remind everyone we are not in a bilateral world, there are third parties. In this case, China may have a zero trade balance globally but still have a trade surplus bilaterally with the US.

He next addressed the relationship between the Stability and Growth Pact and imbalances. Originally, the pact was intended to also affect imbalances and excessive transfers. But, if imbalances were the concern, the one-size-fits-all character of the pact was a mistake as can be seen – just think of the case of Japan which operates a big fiscal deficit and has a current account surplus.

He also argued that the authors took too many of the political constraints as given when they can potentially be removed. Removing political constraints constitutes an important part of political leadership. This is one reason why international organisations exist. Swoboda emphasised the importance of local and global interplay, in which local constraints constitute an excuse for not doing something and in which countries pretend that treaties force them to take actions that they would not take otherwise. This is one case in which some constraints are actually helpful.

Charles Wyplosz, *Professor of International Economics, Graduate Institute of International and Development Studies, Geneva; Director of ICMB*
Charles Wyplosz stated that the authors argue that whenever a spillover is present, an argument for coordination and cooperation is given. He disagreed with this view, arguing that there is only a reason for government intervention in the case of non-pecuniary externalities. In any case, the question is whether there are identified failures and whether the markets do not mediate the spillovers in some way.

This matters for the discussion of good versus bad current account deficits. Referring to Pettis's two-country example, the Germans may decide to save more as a consequence of a higher life expectancy. Running current account surpluses is the only way for them to save collectively. What is missing in Pettis's analysis is that this has market consequences, as the interest rate is driven down in the Eurozone. This is a pecuniary externality which motivates the Spanish people to invest in real estate. There is no market failure here and no argument for policy intervention. Spain may even choose to have a 'fiesta' for ten years and let the next generation pay for its accumulated unproductive debt. What matters is that debts are paid back. The focus should not be on value judgements (bad versus good spending) but on the enforcement mechanism. This is the essence of Rodrik's comparison with the USA, but it is not a case for a fiscal union, only a case for a debt payment mechanism. Since 1841 the USA has enforced an informal no-bailout rule while the Eurozone has ignored its formal no-bailout rule.

Wyplosz wondered whether the G20 is dead, just like the G7, or whether it can be revived. The IMF, too, is being challenged. Many Asian countries have decided not to work closely with the IMF anymore but rather decided to build up their own foreign reserves in order to be able to act outside the IMF framework. Many central banks, including in the developed world, are already bypassing the IMF mechanism: during the crisis, they set up a web of swap agreements, effectively bypassing the IMF and its conditionality.

Last but not least, Wyplosz acknowledged that financial stability was broadly discussed, yet he missed an emphasis on the Basel institutions and on whether Basel III and the Financial Stability Board constitute progress.

Edmond Alphandéry, *Chairman, CNP Assurances, Paris*
Edmond Alphandéry wanted to emphasise that the discussion on current accounts is on sustainability not on spending as such. A current account deficit is much more sustainable when it comes from productive investment which will

allow for repayment in the future. The difficult part, in his opinion, is to draw the border between productive and non-productive investment.

Jeffry Frieden, *Professor of Government, Harvard University, Cambridge*
Jeffry Frieden pointed out that on a domestic level that there are well-established bankruptcy mechanisms accessible to both debtors and creditors. In a world of integrated financial markets and in the presence of current account surpluses and deficits, it is in the interest of both international debtors and creditors to find some mechanism to resolve conflicts over debts that become difficult to service. Leaving aside the aspect of macroeconomic imbalances, it is a mutual problem of mutual interest.

Dani Rodrik, *Rafiq Hariri Professor of International Political Economy, Harvard University, Cambridge*
Dani Rodrik noted that China has been growing due to a combination of repressed interest rates and consumption level, and exchange rate manipulation. Yet consumption growth has been higher than anywhere else. This challenges the view that the Chinese population is actually hurt by these policies. The situation is more subtle. Productivity levels are much higher in the tradable sector. Subsidies encourage low productivity labour to move to high productivity sectors, which generates growth. The self-inflicted wounds view does not describe China's experience correctly.

Discussing China's exchange-rate subsidy, he noted that, as a member of the WTO, China is unable to subsidise the tradable sector directly and therefore seeks an indirect way. A by-product of the exchange-rate subsidy is that imports are taxed, which contributes to the current account surplus. In this view, global governance – in the form of WTO rules – has focused too strongly on preventing beggar-thyself policies in terms of industrial subsidies, and too little on beggar-thy-neighbour policies, which are the macroeconomic imbalances. At the moment, the global government mix is causing more pain to the international system than an easing of the agreement on subsidies would cause.

Responding to Portes, who argued that banks have significant influence in the domestic political sphere, Rodrik suggested that banks had far more influence in Basel. A Dodd-Frank Act could never have been produced in Basel because ultimately there are more stakeholders domestically than internationally.

Michael Pettis, *Senior Associate, Carnegie Endowment, Beijing*
Michael Pettis agreed that the balance of payments is unable to provide information on whether a large capital imbalance is driven by a saving glut in one country or a saving deficit in another one. Analysing the past decade, the US saving rate would not have collapsed if China had not provided the financial capital. Pettis suggested that the driving mechanism should have been differences in interest rates; yet, if a saving glut was involved, this would have caused a reduction in interest rates. The lack of capital was essentially not the driving force of the capital flows into the USA.

He went on to address Rodrik's statement that China essentially subsidises US consumption. Pettis introduced the generosity argument at this stage, although it is essentially a trade-off between employment and consumption growth. If the trade-off works properly, then GDP and household growth increase rapidly after all. The trade-off for China then is not about subsidising US consumption but that its own consumption share is declining. Historically, this investment-driven growth always reaches a stage at which investment starts to be misallocated. In Pettis's opinion this point was reached years ago. So far, every country that had an investment-driven growth miracle ended up in a debt crisis.

Developing the generosity argument, Pettis further stated that China has subsidised US consumption for a very long time, despite being poor. A point has been reached when the USA actually wants to repay; however, this is not in China's interest. This is why he considered that this is not generosity but rather a trade-off between employment and consumption growth.

Yung Chul Park, *Professor, Division of International Studies, Korea University, Seoul*
Yung Chul Park disagreed with the characterisation of an Asian manufacturing subsidy model. It cannot be generalised to all Asian countries as they are strongly diverse in their characteristics. Nor did Park agree with the statement that several countries engage in currency undervaluation. Not all Asian countries were successful in developing an export-led growth strategy, or current account surpluses, through currency undervaluation. Park asked for a clear definition of currency undervaluation and manipulation and a way to measure these. Depending on its final definition, currency manipulation is a bad domestic policy, as it provides an incentive for a misallocation of resources from non-tradable to tradable, with negative implications for consumption.

Park was also concerned about the distinction between beggar-thyself and beggar-thy-neighbour policies. In his opinion, these were not clearly differentiated from one another. Industrial policies, agricultural policies, and export subsidies all have negative cross-border externalities. The difference between beggar-thyself and beggar-thy-neighbour is then just a matter of degree. Particularly in the case of China, it is necessary to identify in what sense China is forced to save.

Regarding the IMF MAP process, Park hoped that a transformation of the IMF into a more independent and transparent body will occur. He foresaw two major obstacles to a successful IMF reform. First, the US veto power and the Europeans' particular interests, with their right to name the head of the organisation. Secondly, the IMF structure is similar to a credit union in which developed countries used to be the lenders and developing countries the borrowers. Although the direction has changed recently, the structure is still intact. Essentially, the IMF is owned by its member states and these member states differ in their individual strength. Therefore, Park asked the authors to provide ideas for reforms

Hans Genberg, *Former Professor, Graduate Institute of International and Development Studies, Geneva*
Hans Genberg focused on current account coordination. The condition that current account balances have to add up to zero does not imply that policy

objectives have to be coordinated in the sense of establishing targets for the current account. The MAP process offers a solution since it provides information on whether current accounts add up under current or prospective policies. If they do not add up under these policies, the need for adjustment is immediately visible. Genberg objected to the statement by Portes that the process is directed towards educating Chinese policymakers. Chinese policymakers do not act irrationally. They are well aware of the international context in which their economy evolves, but they also face complex domestic problems that they must take into account in formulating policies. Regarding the export-led growth model, Genberg disagreed with the report's characterisation of export-led growth as being detrimental to the world economy whereas productivity-enhancing production fragmentation is viewed in positive terms. In his view, if properly interpreted, both are a feature of an international division of labour and should be regarded as beneficial. He also felt that the report was too focused on global imbalances and current policy issues related to these, and not focused enough on what types of coordination or international institutional organisation will be needed in the future once the current problems have been solved and are behind us.

Takatoshi Ito, *Professor, Graduate School of Economics, University of Tokyo, Tokyo*
Takatoshi Ito thought that Spain was essentially a government budget problem, not a current account deficit problem. Fiscal policy has been irresponsible, causing problems that now have to be addressed. He then talked about the analogy between domestic bankruptcy proceedings and their international equivalent, the SDRM (Sovereign Debt Restructuring Mechanism). If a restructuring is necessary, the haircut should be taken by the bondholders and not by Germany, as an analogue to domestic procedures.

Jacques Delpla, *Conseil d'Analyse Économique, Paris*
Jacques Delpla wished to challenge the conventional aspect of the typology of policy coordination. Using the example of education, the authors surely view it as a public good, whereas it can be seen as a regional problem in southern Europe. Whether Spain uses the capital inflows to invest in the educational system or not has strong impacts on neighbouring countries.

Takatoshi Ito, *Professor, Graduate School of Economics, University of Tokyo, Tokyo*
Takatoshi Ito wanted the supporters of Asian export-led growth models to justify it by positive dynamic externalities, which warrant subsidies. China differs from the rest of the Asian tigers in the sense that its income disparity has increased considerably. The income disparity, among other factors, drives the lack of consumption.

He also thought that the report should develop the analysis of currency wars in the light of recent changes. Historically, emerging markets complained about high interest rates in the USA, whereas now they complain about low interest rates.

He described the G20 MAP as neither treaty-based nor related to any agreed-upon discipline. An independent IMF would have the power to write a report without consulting the executive board and would additionally release any report unaware of a member state's complaints.

John Murray, *Deputy Governor, Bank of Canada, Ottawa*
John Murray was puzzled by the distinction between beggar-thy-neighbour and beggar-thyself policies. He did not understand how the authors could accept that countries sometimes adopt beggar-thyself policies given that these constitute a lose-lose outcome; both the domestic and the foreign country lose.

He acknowledged the advances made regarding financial regulation, which were not sufficiently noted by the report. Yet Murray pointed out that challenges remain since the implementation has not been effected.

He thought that currency manipulation can be identified easily in some cases and with difficulty in others. For instance, growth in reserves and the capital controls clearly indicate currency manipulation. The Chinese reluctance to divert from this scheme indicates that it actually worked.

Murray also thought that burying the G20 was premature. Regarding the IMF, its work could be made more efficient by allowing for hard-hitting advice and by allowing for peer-pressure reviews coming from the top rather than from bureaucrats at the bottom level. He concluded that the G20 and the IMF have to be improved and that they should work together; it is not one or the other.

Michael Pettis, *Senior Associate, Carnegie Endowment, Beijing*
Michael Pettis described the Chinese development model as more of an investment-driven economy than an export-driven economy, with the trade surplus only constituting a residual of those policies.

Jeffry Frieden, *Professor of Government, Harvard University, Cambridge*
Jeffry Frieden concluded that the authors' intention was to illustrate what principles are likely to drive global cooperation and international political economy in the future, not to identify specific policies.

References

Artus, P (2012), 'What Causes the Dispersion of Savings Rates between Euro-zone Countries?', *Flash Economics*, No 220. Available at *http://cib.natixis.com/flushdoc.aspx?id=63248* (accessed 2 Apr 2012).

Baldwin, R (2011), 'Trade and Industrialization after Globalization's 2nd Unbundling: How Building and Joining a Supply Chain Are Different and Why It Matters', NBER Working Paper 17716. Available at *http://www.nber.org/papers/w17716* (accessed June 2012).

Bernanke, B S (2005), 'The Global Saving Glut and the U.S. Current Account Deficit', speech at the Sandridge Lecture at the Virginia Association of Economists, Richmond, Virginia. Available at *www.federalreserve.gov/boarddocs/speeches/2005/200503102/default.htm* (accessed June 2012).

Bordo, M D, Eichengreen, B and Irwin, D A (1999), 'Is Globalization Today Really Different than Globalization a Hundred Years Ago?', NBER Working Paper 7195. JEL No F13, F21, F15, N20, E32.

Bown, C and Crowley, M (2012), 'Import Protection, Business Cycles and Exchange Rates: Evidence from the Great Recession', World Bank Policy Research Working Paper 6038, Apr. Washington, DC, World Bank.

Buiter, W and Rahbari, E (2011), 'Global Growth Generators: Moving beyond "Emerging Markets" and "BRIC"', *Global Economics View* 21. Citigroup Global Markets.

Carranza, M (2003), 'Can Mercosur Survive? Domestic and International Constraints on Mercosur', *Latin American Politics and Society* 45 (2), pp 67–103.

Chinn, M and Frieden, J (2011) *Lost Decades: The Making of America's Debt Crisis and the Long Recover,* New York, W. W. Norton.

Chinn, M and Frieden, J (2012), 'How to Save the Global Economy: Whip Up Inflation. Now', *Foreign Policy* (Jan).

Chinn, M, Eichengreen, B and Ito, H (2011), 'A Forensic Analysis of Global Imbalances', NBER Working Paper 17513. Available at *http://www.nber.org/papers/w17513* (accessed June 2012).

Cohen, J and Sabel, C F (2005), 'Global Democracy?', *International Law and Politics* 37 (4), pp 763–97.

Committee on IMF Governance Reform (2009), Final Report, 24 Mar. Washington, DC.

Cooper, R (2005), 'Living with Global Imbalances: A Contrarian View', Peterson Institute Policy Brief 05-3.

De Gregorio, J, Eichengreen, B, Ito, T and Wyplosz, C (1999), 'An Independent and Accountable IMF', *Geneva Reports on the World Economy 1.* Geneva, ICMB.

Dorn, N (2009), 'Financial Market Systemic Regulation: Stability through Democratic Diversity', VoxEU. Available at *http://voxeu.org/index.php?q=node/4411* (accessed June 2012).

Eichengreen, B (1996), *Golden Fetters,* New York, Oxford University Press.

Eichengreen, B (2004), 'What Macroeconomic Measures Are Needed for Free Trade to Flourish in the Western Hemisphere?', *Latin American Politics and Society* 46 (2), pp 1–27.

Eichengreen, B (2009), 'Out of the Box Thoughts about the International Financial Architecture', IMF Working Paper WP/09/116, May.

Eichengreen, B (2011), 'International Policy Coordination: The Long View', NBER Working Paper 17665, Dec.

Eichengreen, B and Baldwin, R (2008), 'What the G20 should Do on November 15th to Fix the Financial System', VoxEU, 10 Nov. Available at *http://voxeu.org/index.php?q=node/2544* (accessed June 2012).

Evenett, S J (2011), 'Trade Tensions Mount: The 10th GTA Report', Global Trade Alert. Available at *http://www.globaltradealert.org/sites/default/files/GTA10_0.pdf* (accessed June 2012).

Fearon, J D (1998), 'Bargaining, Enforcement, and International Cooperation', *International Organization* 52 (2), pp 269–305.

Fischer, S (1999), 'On the Need for an International Lender of Last Resort', *Journal of Economic Perspectives* 13 (4), pp 85–104.

Flandreau, M (1997), 'Central Bank Cooperation in Historical Perspective: A Skeptical View', *Economic History Review New Series* 50 (4), pp 735–63.

Frankel, J (1988), 'Obstacles to International Macroeconomic Policy Coordination', *Studies in International Finance*, No 64. Princeton, Princeton University Press.

Frieden, J (2006), *Global Capitalism*, New York, Norton.

Frieden, J (2009), 'The Crisis and Beyond: Prospects for International Economic Cooperation', Policy Paper 5, PEGGED Collaborative Project, London.

G20 (2008a), 'Action Plan to Implement Principles for Reform', in 'Declaration of the Summit on Financial Markets and the World Economy', Washington, DC, 15 Nov.

G20 (2008b), 'Declaration of the Summit on Financial Markets and the World Economy', Washington, DC, 15 Nov. Available at *http://www.g20.utoronto.ca/2008/2008declaration1115.html* (accessed June 2012).

G20 (2009a), 'G20 Leaders Statement: The Pittsburgh Summit', Pittsburgh, 24/25 Sept. Available at *http://www.g20.utoronto.ca/2009/2009communique0925.html* (accessed June 2012).

G20 (2009b), Communiqué of the Meeting of G20 Finance Ministers and Central Bank Governors, St Andrews, Scotland, 7 Nov. Available at *http://www.g20.utoronto.ca/2009/2009communique1107.pdf* (accessed June 2012).

G20 (2010), 'The Seoul Summit Document', Seoul, 11/12 Nov. Available at *http://www.g20.utoronto.ca/2010/g20seoul-doc.pdf* (accessed June 2012).

G20 (2011a), Final Communiqué of the Meeting of G20 Finance Ministers and Central Bank Governors, Paris, 18/19 Feb. Available at http://www.g20-g8.com/g8-g20/g20/english/for-the-press/news-releases/meeting-of-finance-ministers-and-central-bank.970.html (accessed June 2012).

G20 (2011b), Final Communiqué of Meeting of G20 Finance Ministers and Central Bank Governors, Washington, DC, 15 Apr. Available at *http://www. g8-g20.com/g8-g20/g20/english/for-the-press/news-releases/meeting-of-finance-ministers-and-central-bank.1104.html* (accessed June 2012).

G20 (2011c), 'Final Declaration of the Cannes Summit', Cannes, 4 Nov. Available at *http://www.g20.utoronto.ca/summits/index.html* (accessed June 2012).

Goodhart, C (2012), 'Global Macroeconomic and Financial Supervision: Where Next?', in R Feenstra and A Taylor (eds), *Globalization in an Age of Crisis: Economic Cooperation in the Twenty-First Century*, Chicago, University of Chicago Press, forthcoming.

Goodhart, C A E, Kashyap, A K, Tsomocos, D P and Vardoulakis, A P (2012), 'Financial Regulation in General Equilibrium', University of Chicago Booth Paper No 12-11, Mar.

Grossman, G and Rossi-Hansberg, E (2006), 'The Rise of Offshoring: It's Not Wine for Cloth Anymore', paper for conference for central bankers. Available at *http://www.kansascityfed.org/Publicat/Sympos/2006/PDF/8GrossmanandRossi-Hansberg.pdf* (accessed June 2012).

Hausmann, R and Sturzenegger, F (2006), 'Global Imbalances or Bad Accounting? The Missing Dark Matter in the Wealth of Nations', prepared for 44th Panel Meeting of *Economic Policy* in Helsinki, Finland.

IMF (2006a), 'The Managing Director's Report on Implementing the Fund's Medium-Term Strategy', 5 Apr. Available at *http://www.imf.org/external/np/pp/eng/2006/040506.pdf (accessed June 2012). .*

IMF (2006b), Financial Systems and Economic Cycles, issue of World Economic Outlook (Sept). Available at *http://www.imf.org/external/pubs/ft/weo/2006/02/pdf/weo0906.pdf* (accessed June 2012).

IMF (2010), 'IMF Board Approves Far-reaching Governance Reforms', IMF Survey, 5 Nov, at *http://www.imf.org/external/pubs/ft/survey/so/2010/NEW110510B.htm* (accessed June 2012).

IMF (2011), '2011 Staff Reports for the G-20 Mutual Assessment Process (MAP)'. Available at *http://www.imf.org/external/np/g20/map2011.htm* (accessed June 2012).

IMF (2012), 'The G-20 Mutual Assessment Process (MAP)', Factsheet, 13 Apr. Available at *http://www.imf.org/external/np/exr/facts/g20map.htm* (accessed June 2012).

IMF Independent Evaluation Office (2008), 'Governance of the IMF: An Evaluation', Washington, DC.

International Task Force on Global Public Goods (2006), 'Meeting Global Challenges: International Cooperation in the National Interest', Final Report, Stockholm.

Kenen, P B, Shafer, J, Wicks, N and Wyplosz, C (2004), 'International Economic and Financial Cooperation: New Issues, New Actors, New Responses', *Geneva Report on the World Economy 6*. Geneva, ICMB.

King, M (2011), 'Global Imbalances: The Perspective of the Bank of England', Banque de France, *Financial Stability Review*, No 15 (Feb). Available at *http://*

www.bankofengland.co.uk/publications/Documents/speeches/2011/speech473.pdf (accessed June 2012).

Kitchen, J and Chinn, M (2011), 'Financing US Debt: Is There Enough Money in the World – and at What Cost?', *International Finance* 14 (3),, pp 373–413.

Krueger, A (2001), 'International Financial Architecture for 2002: A New Approach to Sovereign Debt Restructuring', National Economists' Club Annual Members' Dinner Address, Washington DC, American Enterprise Institute.

Krugman, P (2009), 'Macroeconomic Effects of Chinese Mercantilism', blog post. Available at *http://krugman.blogs.nytimes.com/2009/12/31/macroeconomic-effects-of-chinese-mercantilism/* (accessed June 2012).

Leahy , J (2011), '2010 Census Shows Brazil's Inequalities Remain', *Financial Times*, 17 Nov.

Maddison, A (2007), *Contours of the World Economy, 1–2030: Essays in Macroeconomic History*, Oxford, Oxford University Press.

Maddison, A (2010), 'Historical Statistics of the World Economy: 1–2008 AD'. Available at *http://www.ggdc.net/maddison/Historical_Statistics/horizontal-file_02-2010.xls* (accessed June 2012).

McMillan, M S and Rodrik, D (2011), 'Globalization, Structural Change and Productivity Growth', NBER Working Paper 17143, June. Available at *http://www.nber.org/papers/w17143* (accessed June 2012).

Merrouche, O and Nier, E (2010), 'What Caused the Global Financial Crisis? Evidence on the Drivers of Financial Imbalances 1999–2007', IMF Working Paper WP/10/265. Washington, DC, International Monetary Fund.

Mold , A (2010), 'Maddison's Forecasts Revisited: What Will the World Look Like in 2030?', VoxEU. Available at *http://www.voxeu.org/index.php?q=node/5708* (accessed June 2012).

Monterrey Consensus (2003), 'Monterrey Consensus on Financing for Development', text adopted at International Conference on Financing for Development, Monterrey, Mexico, 18/22 Mar. Available at *www.un.org/esa/ffd/monterrey/MonterreyConsensus.pdf (accessed June 2012).*

Obstfeld, M (2012a) 'Does the Current Account Still Matter?', Richard T. Ely Lecture, American Economic Association Annual Meeting, Chicago.

Obstfeld, M (2012b), 'The International Monetary System: Living with Asymmetry', in R Feenstra and A Taylor (eds), *Globalization in an Age of Crisis: Economic Cooperation in the Twenty-First Century*, Chicago, University of Chicago Press, forthcoming.

Obstfeld, M and Rogoff, K (2002), 'Global Implications of Self-Oriented National Monetary Rules', *Quarterly Journal of Economics* 117, pp 503–36.

Obstfeld, M and Rogoff, K (2009), 'Global Imbalances and the Financial Crisis: Products of Common Causes', CEPR Discussion Paper 7606, Centre for Economic Policy Research.

OECD, WTO and UNCTAD (2011), 'Reports on G20 Trade and Investment Measures (Mid-October 2010 to April 2011)', 24 May. Available at *http://www.oecd.org/dataoecd/20/46/47955250.pdf* (accessed June 2012).

Pages, C (ed) (2010), *The Age of Productivity: Transforming Economies from the Bottom Up*, New York, Inter-American Development Bank and Palgrave Macmillan.

Palais-Royale Initiative (2011), 'Reform of the International Monetary System: A Cooperative Approach for the Twenty-First Century', report of group convened by M Camdessus, A Lamfalussy and T Padoa-Schioppa, 8 Feb.

Pew Global Attitudes Project (2007), 'World Publics Welcome Global Trade – But Not Immigration: 47 Nations Pew Global Attitudes Survey', New York, Pew Research Center.

PwC (2011), 'The World in 2050 – The Accelerating Shift of Global Economic Power: Challenges and Opportunities'. Available at *http://www.pwc.com/en_GX/gx/world-2050/pdf/world-in-2050-jan-2011.pdf* (accessed June 2012).

Rajan, R G (2011), 'Currencies Aren't the Problem: Fix Domestic Policy, Not Exchange Rates', *Foreign Affairs* (Mar/Apr).

Rodrik, D (1997), H*as Globalization Gone Too Far?* Washington, DC, Institute for International Economics.

Rodrik, D (2007), *One Economics, Many Recipes: Globalization, Institutions and Economic Growth*, Princeton, Princeton University Press.

Rodrik, D (2008), 'The Real Exchange Rate and Economic Growth', *Brookings Papers on Economic Activity* 2.

Rodrik, D (2010), 'Making Room for China in the World Economy', *American Economic Review*, Papers and Proceedings.

Rodrik, D (2011a), 'The Future of Economic Convergence ', paper prepared for the Jackson Hole meetings.

Rodrik, D (2011b), *The Globalization Paradox*, New York, Norton.

Rodrik, D (2011c), 'Unconditional Convergence', NBER Working Paper 17546.

Rodrik, D (2012), 'Leaderless Global Governance', Project Syndicate, 13 Jan. Available at *http://www.project-syndicate.org/commentary/rodrik66* (accessed June 2012).

Rogoff, K (2011), 'The Second Great Contraction', Project Syndicate, 2 Aug. Available at *http://www.project-syndicate.org/commentary/the-second-great-contraction* (accessed 6 Apr 2012).

Ruggie, J G (2004), 'Reconstituting the Global Public Domain: Issues, Actors, and Practices', European Journal of International Relations 10, pp 499–531.

Sen, A (2009), *The Idea of Justice*, Cambridge, MA, Harvard University Press.

Simmons, B (1997), *Who Adjusts? Domestic Sources of Foreign Economic Policy during the Interwar Years,* Princeton, Princeton University Press

Slaughter, A-M (2004), *A New World Order*, Princeton, Princeton University Press.

Subramanian, A (2011), *Eclipse: Living in the Shadow of China's Economic Dominance*, Washington, DC, Peterson Institute for International Economics.

Truman, E M (2006), 'A Strategy for IMF Reform', Policy Analyses in International Economics, Institute for International Economics, Feb.

UN General Assembly (2000), United Nations Millennium Declaration. Resolution 55/2, adopted 8 Sept. Available at *http://www.un.org/millennium/declaration/ares552e.htm* (accessed June 2012).

US Patent Office (2012), 'US Patent Statistics, 1963–2011', table. Available at *http://www.uspto.gov/web/offices/ac/ido/oeip/taf/us_stat.pdf* (accessed 7 Apr 2012).

Zedillo, E (2006), 'Imbalances Can't Go On Forever', *Forbes Magazine*, 10 July.